Travel
Made Easy

To Lynne

All the best with your planning

Tammy Hawkin

GLOBAL
PUBLISHING
G R O U P

Global Publishing Group
Australia • New Zealand • Singapore • America • London

Travelling
Made Easy

A Step By Step Guide
To Holidays Of A Lifetime

GOLDEN NUGGETS from a Travel Industry Professional

Tarnya Hawkins

First Edition 2015

Copyright © 2015 Tarnya Hawkins

National Library of Australia
Cataloguing-in-Publication entry:

Creator: Hawkins, Tarnya, author.

Title: Travelling Made Easy : A Step By Step Guide To Holidays Of A Lifetime / Tarnya Hawkins.

1st ed.
ISBN: 9781922118691 (paperback)

Subjects:
Travel
Vacations – Planning – Handbooks, manuals, etc

Dewey Number: 910.202

Published by Global Publishing Group
PO Box 517 Mt Evelyn, Victoria 3796 Australia
Email info@GlobalPublishingGroup.com.au

For further information about orders:
Phone: +61 3 9739 4686 or Fax +61 3 8648 6871

Dedicated to my mother Raylee Hawkins
who, at sixteen years of age, left
Australia for New Zealand on a twelve
month working holiday. She instilled in
me a spirit of adventure, a passion for
travelling and a 'let's see what is down
this road' attitude to life and living.

Tarnya Hawkins

Acknowledgements

What a joy it has been to write this book. Hopefully it will inspire you to start planning your next holiday and encourage you on your journey of discovering this amazing world in which we live.

As with any major project, there are a number of very special people who contributed to making this book happen so I'd like to take this opportunity to say "THANK YOU."

Firstly, I'd like to thank my dear friend Di Hillman, who believed in my ability to write this book long before I did. Thank you for the long hours of proofreading and suggestions, especially in the chapter on special diets.

A special thank you to my Mum, Raylee, my brother, Roy and sister-in-law, Amber, for their unconditional love and encouragement and to Stuart and Elizabeth for always making me proud to be your Aunty.

Thank you to Kerri Setch, my friend for over thirty years and one of my first travelling buddies, for your brilliant insight into all things photographic and to Greg Hardacre, for your wisdom and input with all things to do with customs and immigration.

A huge thank you to my mentor, Darren Stephens, to Jackie Stephens and the awesome team at Global Publishing, for your dedication and commitment to this book's success.

As a gift for taking the time to read this book, please use the coupons below any time you would like to travel with me on one of my tours.

$500 OFF
any *Travelling Made Easy* Tour
led by the author, Tarnya Hawkins
* not to be used with any other offer

$500 OFF
any *Travelling Made Easy* Tour
led by the author, Tarnya Hawkins
* not to be used with any other offer

$500 OFF
any *Travelling Made Easy* Tour
led by the author, Tarnya Hawkins
* not to be used with any other offer

$500 OFF
any *Travelling Made Easy* Tour
led by the author, Tarnya Hawkins
* not to be used with any other offer

Table of Contents

Foreword

I sighed with relief as the plane carrying the precious cargo of my two very dear friends raced down the runway in Ketchikan, Alaska, then was suddenly airborne and winging its way towards Seattle. As I watched, it got smaller and smaller in the sky till only a dot remained and then it vanished completely into the clouds. I had just done my very first medical evacuation after a lifetime of travelling and everything had gone very smoothly. Again, I was reminded of the importance of travel insurance. I guess you are wondering about the circumstances behind the medical evacuation that took place. To answer your question, let me tell you how I came to own a travel business that specialises in taking small groups of no more than ten people to exciting locations all around the world.

It seems that in one way or another, my entire life has been spent involved in the travel industry. Both of my parents worked for a company called Roylen Cruises. This company operated out of the tropical town of Mackay in North Queensland and took passengers on a five day cruise to the neighbouring Whitsunday Islands and out to the Great Barrier Reef. Tom McLean, who started the business after World War II, bought a number of Fairmiles which had been used by the Australian Navy, and he refurbished these and turned them into small cruise ships capable of carrying twenty five passengers and eight crew. These were exciting days as people from all over the world came to explore the Great Barrier Reef and the tropical islands. As children, my brother and I got to spend a lot of time on these ships and grew up with the reef and islands as the backdrop to a lot of our childhood adventures. We were both able to drive these ships before we could drive cars. Yes, I know you don't *drive* a ship, you steer it, but as a twelve year old, it had a wheel and therefore it was driven. My brother went on to get his masters ticket and has enjoyed life on the water as the captain of many Australian ships. I continued to work for Roylen Cruises while at high school and eventually became the very first female deckhand in the Whitsunday's. When I wasn't a deckhand I worked as a galley rat [kitchen hand] and after a short stint with an ex navy chef, I knew I also wanted to become a chef.

This led me to Brisbane where I started my apprenticeship under a well known European chef. My training was very much classical French, which was all the rage at the time, and also peeling and preparing more vegetables than I ever want to think about again. About six months into my apprenticeship, an opening came up with Trans Australia Airlines or TAA, as it was more commonly known.

TAA had the contract, through Inflight Catering, to provide all the services to any airline landing at Brisbane Airport, with the exception of Ansett who had their own facilities.

It was during my seven years with Inflight Catering that I not only learnt about amazing foods but started to explore the world beyond Australia. The big perk of working for an airline back in those days was that you got to travel *very* cheaply. We paid just twenty-five percent of any airfare and I took full advantage of this by constantly flying somewhere every time I got a weekend off on my roster. We had a revolving roster where every five weeks you had Thursday and Friday off one week and Saturday and Sunday off the following week. Add to this that we started work at 3.00 a.m. and finished at 11.00 a.m. on the Wednesday and you could swap a shift on Monday to start at 12.00 p.m. So every five weeks I would fly out of the country on Wednesday after work, spend the next four days at my chosen destination and be back in time for work on Monday afternoon. They were crazy days at some of the most amazing destinations you could imagine and I was totally hooked by the travel bug.

My life changed direction seven years after I started with the airlines when I left to work with the Uniting Church in Australia. Australia was to host an International Christian Youth Conference and I had been asked to take on the responsibility of organising this with the most talented team of young people I have ever worked with. We pulled off an amazing conference with a very limited budget, bringing together one thousand, five hundred young people from over forty countries to spend ten days on top of a freezing cold Mt Tamborine in the middle of winter.

When the conference finished I continued to work as a youth and children's worker with the Uniting Church, the Anglican Church and as a chaplain at a local high school. I never lost my love of travel and adventure and those next twelve years were filled with taking young people away on camps, ski trips, house boat cruises, schoolies weeks and international holidays of a lifetime. Once I turned forty I decided it was time for a younger person to take over my role of working with young people and I turned my attention to setting up a catering company.

My two great passions have always been travel and food and I was forever dragging friends all around the world to experience both. It was only natural that this would evolve into the travel business that we own today. Affiliated with Integrity Travel, Travelling Made Easy is quickly becoming the leader of small group tour companies here in Australia and as we expand into other parts of the world, our company is beginning to be known as one with integrity and the promise that we do what we say and indeed you will experience holidays of a lifetime. I personally lead at least five or six of our tours each year and often these will be in Canada and the USA, including Alaska and Hawaii. I have spent a lifetime travelling through the USA and Canada and love to show new friends what beautiful and friendly countries these are once you leave the cities behind.

This brings me back to our medical evacuation. After more than thirty years of travelling, it was only last year that we had our first injury when one of our travellers, who also happens to be a dear friend, slipped on some out of place ice and broke her arm just below her shoulder ball joint. The first doctor we saw strapped her arm and shoulder and with some medication thought it would be fine for her to continue on with the tour. By the time we had reached Alaska, the strapping was coming loose and we saw another doctor, just to get the strapping redone. As can sometimes happen with differing opinions, his recommendation was that she return home immediately for surgery. The outcome, once back in Australia, was that she did not need surgery and she could have continued with us. Another lesson learned and tip to pass on is that any time you have strapping done, take a photo, so you know how to do it again if it comes loose. I'm also happy to report that she and her husband are doing another trip with me this year. You can check out all of my tours for this year by visiting our website.

As I mention in the introduction, the first few chapters will take you step by step through planning any holiday or short break that you may like to organise for yourself. The remaining chapters will help you leave home feeling confident that you have everything under control, whether travelling by yourself, with family or friends or travelling as part of a tour group. So let's get started.

Introduction

> 66 *Holidays....the very word makes us feel happy. We can see the photos and we can hear the stories but we need to be there to feel the experience.* 99

Tarnya Hawkins

Travelling can be easy, stress free and lots of fun if you sit down and do some planning in the beginning. In this planning phase you will decide on the places you want to visit, the things you would like to see and do, experiences you would like to share with your family or travelling companions, when you will be away from home, how long you will be away from home and roughly how much your holiday will cost.

I am going to take you step by step through the whole holiday planning process that I use for all of the holidays and tours that I run, either here in Australia or anywhere else in the world. For the purpose of this book, in the first few chapters I will be showing you how I put together a holiday to the United States and Canada. These easy to follow steps can be used for holidays to any country in the world as well as for holidays within your own country. They can be used any time you leave home, even for a weekend getaway.

Within this book are the tools you will need to create awesome times away from home. There will be templates that you can print for your own personal use, there will be websites that you can visit and a list of resources that you may find helpful. Also, take your pen and as you read through the pages, circle or highlight anything that you find helpful and may need to come back to. For a free copy of all the templates used in this book, go to www. travellingmadeeasy.com.au. You can print whatever you need to get you started on planning your holiday.

I look forward to meeting you somewhere in the world and hearing where you have travelled to; those wonderful stories of the places, the people, the food, the culture and the experiences we share as travellers.

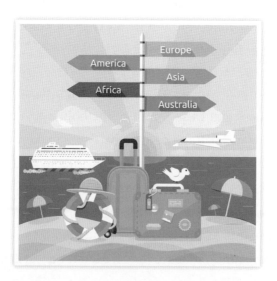

CHAPTER 1

WHERE DO I WANT TO GO AND HOW DO I WANT TO TRAVEL?

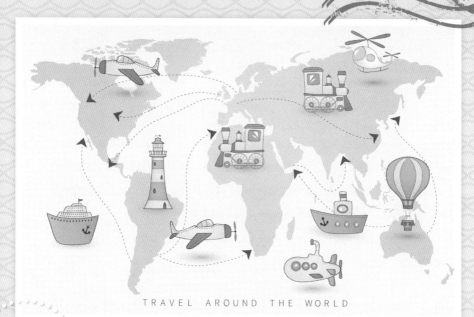

TRAVEL AROUND THE WORLD

CHAPTER 1

WHERE DO I WANT TO GO AND HOW DO I WANT TO TRAVEL?

> 66 *Twenty years from now you will be more disappointed by the things you didn't do than by the ones you did do. So throw off the bowlines and sail away from the safe harbour. Catch the trade winds in your sails. Explore. Dream. Discover.* 99

Mark Twain

It was a very hot Australian afternoon in Brisbane, Queensland and I was sitting with my housemate and her sixteen year old daughter in the shade of our pergola, with the hope of catching a cool breeze. There and then we decided to plan a holiday in the northern hemisphere to escape the heat of, at least part of, one sweltering Australian summer.

Our biggest problem was that there were so many options to choose from including a driving tour of the United Kingdom visiting England, Scotland and Wales with a side trip to Ireland, an organised coach tour through Europe that covered a number of different countries or a river cruise down one of the iconic rivers in Germany. As well as getting an apartment in Paris and doing lots of day trips, skiing in Switzerland, seeing the Christmas lights of Norway, spending time on the Amalfi Coast in Italy or taking a food tour through Tuscany. Then there was cruising scenic Scandinavia and its Fjords, enjoying endless sunsets at Santorini, walking along the Great Wall of China, visiting the pyramids in Egypt, enjoying the beauty of Croatia or staying in an over water bungalow in the Maldives.

We finally decided we wanted to visit the United States of America and while we were there add on a trip to Canada. The reason we picked the United States was that it was a lifelong dream of my housemate to experience a white Christmas and I wanted to ride a snowmobile through Yellowstone National Park in winter.

We looked at a map of the United States and talked together about the most important things that each of us wanted to see and do.

In no particular order, our list looked something like this:

- *Go to Disneyland*

- *Walk across the Golden Gate Bridge in San Francisco*

- *Visit an Amish community*

- *Ride a snowmobile through Yellowstone National Park*

- *Watch the ball drop on New Year's Eve in New York City*

- *See Niagara Falls*

- *Visit friends who live in Kentucky*

- *Listen to jazz music in New Orleans*

- *Go snow skiing on Christmas Day*

- *Visit Sea World in San Diego*

- *Drive all the way to Key West*

Looking at this master list we divided it into three smaller lists. The things that we **had** to see or do, the things that we would have **liked** to see or do and the things that would have been **nice** to do but that we were willing to take off the list if we couldn't fit it all in.

The new lists looked like this:

Would Have To Do

- *Visit friends who live in Kentucky*

- *Go to Disneyland*

- *Ride a snowmobile through Yellowstone National Park*

- *Go snow skiing on Christmas Day*

Would Like To Do

- *Listen to jazz music in New Orleans*

- *Visit Sea World in San Diego*

- *Visit an Amish community*

- *See Niagara Falls*

Would Be Nice To Do

- *Watch the ball drop on New Year's Eve in New York City*

- *Drive all the way to Key West*

- *Walk across the Golden Gate Bridge in San Francisco*

The next thing was to decide when to go. We decided that we would need a couple of years to save up for this trip. It was now January. Emma would finish Year Twelve at high school the following year in November. In the week following a student finishing high school here in Australia, the majority go off with their friends and without their parents, on a week long holiday called "Schoolies Week." She was more than happy to have a five week "Schoolies" in the United States. So the date was set. School finished on the Friday and we would fly out on the Saturday. Travelling at the end of November, through December and into early January would mean that we would miss a chunk of the hot southern hemisphere summer and enjoy time in the northern hemisphere winter.

At this stage of our planning we would fly from Brisbane to Los Angeles where we would pick up a rental car and drive wherever we wanted to go, ending up back in Los Angeles to fly home.

As I sat thinking about how easy this sounded, my thoughts turned to earlier trips I had taken. A couple of years before, I had visited Europe for a milestone birthday. I decided not to have a birthday party but rather go to Paris instead. Going all the way from Brisbane to Paris was a long way and so we decided to extend the time and see Europe while we were there. Our flight on that trip was from Brisbane to London, via Sydney and Bangkok, which is a very long flight. If at all possible, take a break along the way. We stopped over in Bangkok for a couple of days and this break was both enjoyable and interesting as we learnt a little about the culture of Thailand. Stopovers are often offered by the airlines with no extra charge on the price of your airfare. There are many hotels near the airport if you want to be based there or an easy taxi ride will take you into the heart of the city. It is always a good idea to have this accommodation booked before you leave home. Most taxi drivers speak English and so getting around is quite simple. Make sure you have some local currency with you before you get in the taxi and make sure it is a legitimate taxi not a clone. When taking a taxi, insist on them using their meter if they have one. If they don't have one, negotiate the price before you go with them or don't use them. Other good stopover destinations on the way to London are Singapore, Dubai or even Hong Kong. Your choice of stopover destination however, will be determined by the airline you choose to fly with.

> 66
> *Stopovers are often offered by the airlines with no extra charge on the price of your airfare.* 99

While I think nothing about driving all over the United States, it is not something I would do in Europe. The United Kingdom would certainly be fine as their rules are similar to ours and you can at least understand the road signs. I would not suggest that anyone drive in Europe unless they can at least understand the language of the road signs. In fact, for any first time visit to Europe, where your time is limited, it is wiser to take a guided tour. This is exactly what we did, travelling through a number of different countries on a twenty-one day tour that departed from London and finished in Athens. While our visit to each country was brief, we did have the benefit of learning as much as possible within the safety and comfort of our coach and with the guidance of our very knowledgeable tour director who spoke five languages. We did not have to worry about one thing apart from enjoying ourselves and taking lots of photos. We also got a clear indication of places and countries we would like to visit again and those that we probably would not return to.

Travelling will always be easier in countries that speak the same languages as the ones that you know. This should not stop you from exploring other fascinating areas of the world but you will just need to plan a little more and even learn the language if you have the time. Saying you need to learn the language does not necessarily mean that you have to speak fluently like a local but to know phrases or words that will help you navigate through the country in safety and comfort. There are also a number of excellent translating apps you can use on your phone or gadgets that you can carry in your pocket or bag. For any country, you need to research the culture, so that you stay out of trouble and do not offend anyone. This can be as simple as covering your head in certain temples to not touching the head of anyone in some of the Pacific Island Nations. Pointing can also be offensive and certainly, using coarse language is always frowned upon.

I had the misfortune of learning this the hard way on a particular trip to Thailand in my early twenties. With a little research I could have learnt that pointing my feet at someone is considered very rude, as is pointing your feet at Buddha statues. I usually sit with my legs crossed so I offended many people without even knowing it. You must never touch the head or hair of anyone and this includes playfully ruffling the hair of a child. Pointing is also considered very rude. If you must indicate to someone do so by lifting your chin in their direction. Do not disrespect the King of Thailand, who is very much loved by the Thai people. Doing so, will certainly mean time in prison with the option of the death penalty. Always return the prayer like gesture of the hands held in front and your head slightly bowed called a 'Wai.' Not doing so is considered very rude as only the King and monks do not have to return this gesture. Show utmost respect to monks and be aware that women are not permitted to touch them or their clothing or hand anything to them. You should always wait until monks have eaten first at any gathering where they are present. Always remove your shoes before entering a temple or a house. Never get angry or yell in public in Thailand and always remember to smile. Each country has its own set of rules and customs and it would be wise to look these up on the internet before you leave home.

When we decided to go to Europe and take a guided tour, there were also other considerations to make, such as how long we would like to be on tour and which itinerary really appealed to us. There will be so many choices you can make for any trip to Europe. By visiting any travel agency you will be able to pick up brochures offered by the bigger tour companies. Take a good look at the itineraries to find the ones that appeal to you most. Then take a look at the price and see what you are getting for that price. What is the standard of the hotels you will be staying in? Where are those hotels situated in relation to the cities you are visiting? What meals are included? Does the cost include entry to all the attractions you will visit? Is there a tour director and will the commentary be done in English or another language of your choice? Does the cost include porterage of your suitcases? Does the tour company use local guides for more in depth exploration of a particular area? Does the cost include all transportation and is tipping or gratuities included? What is the pace of the tour and how much walking is involved? By answering these questions you will discover what is important to you on a guided tour. You may prefer, for example, to pay less and be on a tour that only stays in three star accommodations or you may not mind staying further out of town. For others, it will be more important to stay in the centre of a town so that you are able to walk around on your own and check out the sights that interest you most in your free time. If you are older and have trouble walking, you may be looking for a tour that is leisurely paced.

There has been a boom in the number of people who now prefer to see Europe while on a river cruise. River cruising has a lot of benefits such as just unpacking the once and hanging your clothes and stowing your gear in the cabin you know you will have for at least the next seven days and sometimes even longer. Cabins or staterooms, as they are called on board, tend to be very luxurious and most have a view out of oversized windows to watch the changing scenery as you cruise along. You can also opt for a stateroom or suite with your own personal balcony, where you can sit and watch the world go by. River cruising ships are known as 'floating hotels' and usually offer all the amenities you would expect to find in a four or five star hotel including attentive staff who will take care of your every need. Because river cruising ships are much smaller than ocean cruising ships the number of passengers on board may vary from fifty to two hundred depending on which ship you choose. You will not feel like part of a larger multitude but rather enjoy the intimate experience of small ship cruising and a crew who knows your name, can help you plan your activities ashore and even baristas who remember how you take your coffee. You will not find flashy casinos or theatres on board but rather like minded travellers you can have meaningful conversations with.

Each morning you will wake up to something new, whether that is a new country, new city or town or new scenery on the shore line. Each day you will have the opportunity to experience local life and customs as you stop at each port for several hours before moving on. You can do this either on your own or on a prearranged guided tour organised by your cruise coordinator. These shore excursions will often use local guides who know the very best places to take you and things to show you that you may miss if travelling on your own.

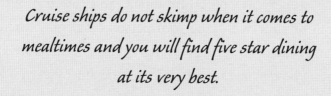

Cruise ships do not skimp when it comes to mealtimes and you will find five star dining at its very best.

When you return to your ship at night you will be amazed by the gourmet meals you are served. Cruise ships do not skimp when it comes to mealtimes and you will find five star dining at its very best. Some cruise ships offer local wines and beer as part of your overall package and meals are generally matched in part to the local surroundings, so you could enjoy escargot with a full bodied red while cruising through Bordeaux, the much heartier Bavarian foods while cruising through southern Germany or the southern soul food on a Mississippi river cruise in the United States.

River cruising is not just limited to Europe, although that is possibly the most popular. You can cruise the iconic Rhine, Seine, Danube and Rhone waterways of Europe or be introduced to the

Orient as you cruise along the Mekong. There is the Yangtze in China, the Nile in Egypt, the Amazon and Congo Rivers and of course the mighty Mississippi in the United States. Whichever waterway you choose to explore you will do so at a leisurely pace, as you sit back and savour the sights from your private balcony or with others on the spacious sun deck.

Others prefer to see Europe using the train network. This can be quite confusing at times, especially with countries, towns and railway stations spelt in the local language. There are local trains where you can just turn up at the station and board, while other trains will require you to make a reservation. All high speed trains require a reservation in either first or second class. You must also fill in your travelling forms very carefully. My suggestion for trains is that you need to have plenty of time to spare as this is not a quick way to travel. You must also do your homework with the train timetables so you know exactly what type of train you need to travel on. Rail passes can sometimes be confusing and not always the cheapest alternative.

Some companies offer train travel as part of the overall holiday package and do all the hard work of providing timetables and finding out which trains to catch. The Rocky Mountaineer in Canada is perhaps the most well known however, there are many other amazing train journeys that you can take. The Blue Train, widely regarded as one of the world's most luxurious trains, takes you on an unforgettable twenty-eight hour luxury ride from Pretoria to Cape Town in South Africa, while the Ghan in Australia travels through the outback from Darwin to Adelaide. The Indian Pacific travels for four days and three nights in the most indulgent way to experience the vastness of Australia, from Sydney to Perth. Other luxury trains include the Oriental Express, which travels from Singapore through Malaysia to Bangkok, the Golden Eagle Trans Siberian Express, travelling on a twelve night journey from Moscow to Vladivostok and the Royal Scotsman, with a four night, three day journey for just thirty-six passengers from Edinburgh across the Highlands to the fishing town of Mallaig on the scenic northwest coast. Switzerland has the Glacier Express and the United States has the California Zephyr Superliner, which travels nearly four thousand kilometres between Chicago and Emeryville near San Francisco in about fifty-four hours and is regarded as one of North America's most scenic train trips. In South America you can travel for just over three hours from Poroy, near Cusco, to Machu Picchu, six days a week on a journey through some of the Andes' most breathtaking scenery on the Hiram Bingham. At Machu Picchu you disembark to take a five hour tour and then head back to Cusco on the same train while enjoying a fine Andean dinner.

The finest of all train trips is perhaps the Simplon Orient Express. From London's Victoria Station to Gare de l'Est in Paris where French chefs prepare Michelin grade menus of lobster, scallops and caviar for your dinner. The train travels through the night while you peacefully sleep and when you awake refreshed in the morning you will be served breakfast in bed before you arrive in Venice.

Bus-A-Bout, a hop on-hop off bus company, offers a simple way to travel through Europe using buses instead of trains. They also offer a number of tours to travel with young like-minded people. The bus pick up points are often near youth hostels. My god-daughter and her friend travelled all through the United Kingdom and Europe using Bus-A-Bout point to point services as well as doing specific tours with them. They had the most wonderful time and made many new friends from right across the world. You can opt to take an organised tour, do flexi trips or loops with the Bus-A-Bout Company.

Another fairly stress-free way to travel is ocean cruising on a cruise ship. Again this is an 'unpack only once' kind of holiday with more activities, food and destinations than you could ever imagine. Cruising has certainly come a long way in recent years with choices between large cruise ships that traverse the globe to smaller more intimate cruise ships that align themselves with a particular area.

I have taken a number of cruises over the years and each has been different. I have cruised through the Greek Islands, the Caribbean,

South America, Alaska Inside Passage and through the Panama Canal. All have been breathtakingly beautiful and are a great way to travel if you like a slower pace. The pace on board can be as relaxing or as busy as you like, with activities from sunrise to late at night each and every day. Getting on board at the start of your cruise is usually a fairly easy procedure. However, give yourself plenty of time as it can be a lengthy process. Drop your luggage off at the designated area, line up, fill out a health form, check in with passport and credit card for all onboard expenditures as all cruise ships operate on a cashless system. This means that anything you buy on the cruise ship including onshore excursions will be charged to the credit card used at check-in. You also have the option of paying this account with either cash or a different credit card before leaving the ship at the end of your cruise.

You will be given a key card to your cabin which also acts as your security pass when you go ashore and return to the ship and also the charge card for any expenses incurred while on board. It is a great idea to buy a lanyard that you can wear around your neck and attach this key card to it. This is the easiest way to keep it in a safe place without the possibility of losing it and the quickest way to find it when you need to use it.

My mother and I enjoyed a wonderful cruise from New York to Los Angeles when the Norwegian Jewel was being repositioned from Europe, where she had spent the northern hemisphere winter, to

Alaska for the northern hemisphere summer. We crossed from the Atlantic Ocean to the Pacific Ocean through the Panama Canal. This was something I had wanted to do since hearing my father speak about doing this on the HMAS Perth, while serving in World War II. Repositioning cruises can also be quite economical and usually do not have a full complement of passengers as they can be longer cruises than the normal seven to ten days. You do tend to get to know your fellow passengers better on a longer cruise. This, for me, has led to forming wonderful friendships with people from all over the world whom I have kept in touch with and visited whenever possible.

I met a lovely brother and sister on one cruise who travel fairly extensively throughout the world and they do this via house exchanges. They particularly like France and will often do a house exchange for a week or two. The house exchange can sometimes come with a car and phone so you can easily get around. He recommends this as a great way to get a more in-depth feel for one particular place and also make lifelong friends. Go to www. houseexchange.com if you would like to check this out.

We also work closely with a company called Sailing Adventures, who take small group tours on wonderful sailing adventures to exotic locations around the world. You can check out their website at www.sailingadventures.com.au.

Holidays can be just as exciting in your own country. I have travelled all over Australia using various methods such as driving a car, riding a motorbike, travelling by train and even driving coach tours and I have just scratched the surface of the abundance that there is to see and do. Many Australians, once they retire, have a dream of buying a four wheel drive vehicle and caravan and taking off on a circumnavigation of our amazing country. As an alternative to this, there is an amazing family run company based in Brisbane, called Cross Country Tours, who take travellers on an exploration of Australia in the comfort of their air conditioned and very roomy luxury coaches. They have knowledgeable and friendly drivers and hosts who take care of your every need while explaining everything that you are seeing with insightful commentary. Each year they have one coach that goes all the way around Australia and you can either choose to do the whole trip or to meet the coach in a specific location to do just a certain portion of the route. They offer lots of exciting getaways for day trips and short holidays for those who prefer to travel in a group by coach. I would highly recommend that if you are planning on taking an extended coach trip as part of your holiday plans, that you take a couple of day trips first, so you know what to expect with coach travel. You can check them out at www.crosscountrytours.com.au

Enough daydreaming of past holidays; I had some work to do in mapping out the sequence of places we would visit during our holiday to the United States and Canada.

CHAPTER 2

ITINERARY PLANNING

CHAPTER 2

ITINERARY PLANNING

> 66 *We live in a wonderful world that is worth exploring and discovering and in doing so we discover more about ourselves.* 99

Tarnya Hawkins

I grabbed a writing pad, pencil, eraser and map of America and Canada and sat down with a cool drink. The first thing I did was write the date of each day we would be away on a separate line, down one side of the writing pad. This was just for my visual rough copy that would be transferred to a spreadsheet later on. Many years later, based on that first trip, I now use a spreadsheet program right from the start, as this saves me a lot of time and I can change things quickly and easily.

Setup your PLANNING STAGE spreadsheet on your computer or use a pad and pen and start to set your holiday of a lifetime in motion.

Below is an example of the first seven days. Ours looked something like this:

24th November

25th November

26th November

27th November

28th November

29th November

30th November

I then added where we would be for each of those days:

24th November   *Brisbane to Los Angeles*

25th November   *Anaheim*

26th November   *Anaheim*

27th November   *Anaheim*

28th November   *Drive from Anaheim to San Diego*

29th November   *San Diego*

30th November   *Drive from San Diego to Las Vegas*

Next was to look at each area we would be visiting and see if there were particular things we would like to do there and then add these to the spreadsheet.

24th November	Brisbane to Los Angeles Drive from Los Angeles to Anaheim	
25th November	Anaheim	Disneyland
26th November	Anaheim	Disneyland
27th November	Anaheim	Disneyland
28th November	Drive from Anaheim to San Diego Stop at San Juan Capistrano	
29th November	San Diego	Sea World
30th November	Drive from San Diego to Las Vegas	

By this early stage of planning I realised we were not going to see everything we wanted to and it was in fact silly to try and squash so much into a six week time frame. We decided to take Canada and Florida out of the plan and do those areas on another trip.

With this rough idea of what we wanted to do it was time to work out how much this might cost. We had nearly two years in which to save and if we could come up with a plan, our holiday would be paid for before we went. We did not want to pay for the holiday on a credit card and then be stuck paying it off for years to come.

Getting a rough idea of the price early in the planning would also help us determine if in fact we could stay for six weeks. If the cost was higher than we thought we had the option early in this planning stage to either shorten the length of the time we would be away or determine if there was an amount in dollars that we were happy to put on our credit card and pay off later.

The first thing was to look at the cost of flights. We were two years out from our travel date and airlines will only post prices twelve months in advance so I started to look at the flights we would possibly take and use the present price as an indication. The first thing I noticed was that flights were cheaper if you travelled on a Tuesday or Wednesday and far more expensive on Fridays and Sundays. We got a rough idea of how much our flights would cost and added a bit more for the usual yearly increase.

I looked up the room rate for hotels where we would like to stay and again got a rough idea of how much this might cost per night. At this point in our planning we also got a rough idea of how much travel insurance would cost and the rough cost for all the attractions we wanted to see. This process was very time consuming and I spent hours on the internet.

It was worth every minute though as I took notes on each attraction including cost of entry, what days they were open and what hours they operated. I also wrote down the physical address and any other information that we might find helpful. Next was to work out how much it would cost to hire a rental car for six weeks and the extra cost for a one way rental. I did a rough addition of how many miles we would travel and what I thought fuel might cost. Lastly, I added in how much we thought we would spend on food each day.

Once I had added all these costs together, we had a starting point of how much we would need to save. As I mentioned, this was a longer process than I first thought and something I could only do on weekends or my spare time at night after work. By the time I had all this information together it was nearly the end of April. On the 29th of April we put away our first weekly installment of $260. We would leave in eighty-four weeks and our goal was to save $22,000, which would entirely pay for our six week holiday.

Once we were within the twelve month window we found a great deal with Hawaiian Airlines that was too good to pass up. So, with an adjustment to the date we would leave and by flying through Hawaii, we would save a substantial amount of money. When we spoke to our travel agent about this, she suggested we have our money available to pay for our flights and wait to take advantage of visiting a Travel Expo that was coming up. This was great advice as we got a fantastic deal that was only offered at the Travel Expo.

Our itinerary changed many times over the next twelve months as we added things in and took things out. I was now also adding in where we would stay each night once I had made the booking. With our flights now secured with Hawaiian Airlines we decided to stay in Hawaii, both on the way there and when returning to Australia. We knew the lead up to getting away would be crazy with a thousand last minute things to do and we would be very tired, so we changed our Itinerary to include five days in Honolulu to just relax and enjoy being on holidays before we started our road trip. I would highly recommend having at least one or two totally relaxing days as you start your holidays. We had also decided that we didn't want to be driving to a new destination every night but rather have time in each place to enjoy the scenery, the people and the local culture. Some days of course just needed to be travel days.

The other thing that changed our itinerary was that as we started to save for our holiday, we seemed to find more ways to save money. Each time we saved more, we were able to add more days to our holiday. Another factor to change our itinerary was that I had stumbled across a program called the Go OAHU Card. This card gave you a multitude of attractions you could visit for one low price. You could choose how many days you would like the card for and this determined the price. We went with the five day card because we gained a day by going to Honolulu as we crossed the International Date Line. By purchasing the card we got to experience things we perhaps wouldn't have tried on our own.

Our new itinerary was beginning to look like this:

26th November	Brisbane to Honolulu	Resort Quest	
27th November	Honolulu	Resort Quest	
28th November	Honolulu	Resort Quest	
29th November	Honolulu	Resort Quest	
30th November	Honolulu	Resort Quest	
1st December	Honolulu to San Francisco	Staying with Chris	
2nd December	San Francisco	Staying with Chris	
3rd December	San Francisco	Staying with Chris	
4th December	San Francisco	Staying with Chris	
5th December	San Francisco to Morro Rock	Blue Sail Inn	

We had two options of flights from Honolulu to either Los Angeles or to San Francisco. We had good friends in San Francisco, who, once they found out we were visiting the United States, asked us to come and stay with them. We stayed with them for four days and got a local perspective on San Francisco as well as enjoyed their company.

On the last afternoon of our stay, we were taken to the airport to pick up our rental car. When we arrived at the desk, the clerk mentioned that he had a hybrid car available for an additional cost. Thinking he was just trying to up-sell, I declined the offer. However, he said we would save far more in fuel than the extra rental cost and he was right. Our fuel costs for the trip were much lower than we had budgeted for. If you are going to be travelling long distances, always try to get a hybrid car.

> *If you are going to be travelling long distances, always try to get a hybrid car.*

We had decided to drive the beautiful coast road between San Francisco and Los Angeles taking our time and stopping overnight along the way. I had found in my research, a great little fishing village called Morro Bay which seemed like the perfect spot to spend the night. We were not disappointed.

We were making our way to Anaheim to spend time at Disneyland and we would be driving through Los Angeles. As there were a number of things to see and do in Los Angeles we decided it would make more sense to stay for a couple of days on the way through and take in the sights before driving further south. We would then have five days in Anaheim using a three day Disneyland pass and having the other two days to look around the area. Once again we used the Go LA Card and found other attractions that interested us both in Los Angeles and Anaheim. One such attraction was a tour you could take on the Queen Mary. Another was a San Diego Cruise. By checking out the attractions or things that we wanted to see or do, in each of the particular areas that we would stay, really helped us to determine how long we would actually stay in each place. This process also allowed us to book our accommodation accordingly. Wherever possible I booked accommodation that would have a no fee cancellation policy if our plans were to change. This simple act saved us a lot of money later on in our trip when the weather turned bad and roads were closed.

We added to our Itinerary:

6th December	Morro Rock to LA	Holiday Inn Airport	
7th December	Los Angeles	Holiday Inn Airport	
8th December	Anaheim	Super 8 Disneyland	
9th December	Anaheim	Super 8 Disneyland	
10th December	Anaheim	Super 8 Disneyland	
11th December	Anaheim	Super 8 Disneyland	

12th December	Anaheim	Super 8 Disneyland	
13th December	Anaheim to San Diego	Holiday Inn Express	
14th December	San Diego	Holiday Inn Express	
15th December	San Diego	Holiday Inn Express	

Again we used the Go Card for the attractions we wanted to visit while in San Diego as this was proving far more economical than paying for each attraction individually. We also had the opportunity to experience things that we might not normally have picked.

We had now come to a point in our itinerary where we didn't really know where we wanted to go next. We did know that we wanted to spend Christmas in Jackson Hole, Wyoming and that we would like to be there for seven days. We also decided that we would celebrate the New Year with our friends in Kentucky and that it would be a three day drive from Jackson Hole, Wyoming to Pikeville, Kentucky. There were ten days from when we would leave San Diego to Christmas Day. So we filled in the part of the itinerary with the things that we knew we wanted to do.

16th December			
17th December			
18th December			
19th December			
20th December			
21st December	Jackson Hole	Ranch Inn	
22nd December	Jackson Hole	Ranch Inn	
23rd December	Jackson Hole	Ranch Inn	
24th December	Jackson Hole	Ranch Inn	
25th December	Jackson Hole	Ranch Inn	
26th December	Jackson Hole	Ranch Inn	
27th December	Jackson Hole	Ranch Inn	
28th December			
29th December			
30th December	Arrive Pikeville		

As we jiggled with the different options we could take, it was finally decided that we would leave San Diego and travel north east to Las Vegas where we would stay the night before driving to the Grand Canyon. From there we would drive to Cortez so we could visit the ruins of Mesa Verde, the fascinating cliff dwellings of the indigenous Puebloan people before they abandoned them in 1300. A drive through the Rocky Mountains would have us staying

in Glenwood Springs for two days before we needed to arrive in Jackson Hole for Christmas. We would also have an indulgence and stay at the Venetian Resort in Las Vegas as a special treat. We were not sure where we wanted to stay at the Grand Canyon and whether this would be at the Grand Canyon itself or at the nearby town of Williams. The same thing applied for Cortez, so we left that open to find accommodation when we got there.

16th December	San Diego to Las Vegas	Venetian Resort
17th December	Las Vegas to Grand Canyon	
18th December	Grand Canyon to Cortez	
19th December	Cortez to Glenwood Springs	Clarion Collection
20th December	Glenwood Springs	Clarion Collection

In looking at the maps on how to get from Jackson Hole to Pikeville we discovered that by travelling through South Dakota we could visit both Mt Rushmore and the Crazy Horse Memorial. As we didn't want to rush these two amazing places we changed our date of departure from Jackson Hole to one day earlier, giving us four days for the drive to Kentucky and we didn't book any accommodation because we really didn't know how long the drive would actually take or where we would be each night. Our itinerary was just a guide.

27th December	Jackson Hole to Deadwood		
28th December	Deadwood to Omaha		
29th December	Omaha to Louisville		
30th December	Louisville to Pikeville		

Our original plan was to spend five days with our friends in Pikeville, Kentucky and then fly back to San Francisco where we would take the flight home via Hawaii, where we would have a one night stopover. However, as I mentioned earlier, we started to save more money and were able to add extra days to our holiday of a lifetime. We had now added an extra twenty six days.

We went back to our original list and added in a visit to an Amish community, Niagara Falls, Martha's Vineyard and New York City.

31st December	Pikeville		
1st January	Pikeville		
2nd January	Pikeville		

3rd January	Pikeville		
4th January	Pikeville to Washington DC	Howard Johnson	
5th January	Washington DC	Howard Johnson	
6th January	Washington DC to Lancaster	Amish View Inn	
7th January	Lancaster	Amish View Inn	
8th January	Lancaster to Niagara Falls		
9th January	Niagara Falls to Point Porpoise		
10th January	Point Porpoise to Boston		
11th January	Boston to Newport		
12th January	Newport to New York	Salisbury Hotel	
13th January	New York	Salisbury Hotel	
14th January	New York	Salisbury Hotel	
15th January	New York	Salisbury Hotel	
16th January	New York	Salisbury Hotel	

We would drop off our rental car in New York City as we would not need it anymore and then fly to Orlando where we would pick up another car to travel around Florida. If we flew from Miami to New Orleans rather than driving across, we would save time and money because there would be no drop off fee on the car if left in Florida. We also left accommodation off our schedule in Florida because we wanted to explore the area and not be tied down by having to be at a certain place at a certain time. I have never taken this liberty with accommodation in New York, always preferring to have this in place before I arrive. I have stayed at the Salisbury Hotel on most visits to New York as I find it quite central and within easy walk of both Times Square and Central Park.

We then added in the final stage of our holiday.

17th January	New York to Mt Dora		
18th January	Mt Dora		
19th January	Mt Dora to Key West		
20th January	Key West to Miami		

21st January	Miami to New Orleans	Holiday Inn French Quarter	
22nd January	New Orleans	Holiday Inn French Quarter	
23rd January	New Orleans	Holiday Inn French Quarter	
24th January	New Orleans to San Francisco	Staying with Chris	
25th January	San Francisco	Staying with Chris	
26th January	San Francisco	Staying with Chris	
27th January	San Francisco	Staying with Chris	
28th January	San Francisco to Honolulu	Resort Quest Banyan	
29th January	Honolulu	Resort Quest Banyan	
30th January	Honolulu	Resort Quest Banyan	
31st January	Honolulu to Brisbane		
1st February	Void		
2nd February	Arrive Brisbane		

We also had friends in Florida, who, when they knew we were coming to visit, asked us to stay with them in Mt Dora. It took a little bit of work to make the itinerary flow by adding these extra flights in but we eventually had everything included. We were warned to only stay in the French Quarter of New Orleans and not to venture away from that area as the crime rate and violence is high elsewhere in the city. This is still the case today. We would finish our holiday with our good friend Chris, in San Francisco and a couple of days in Hawaii to rest and reflect on our amazing holiday. We lost a day flying back to Australia over the International Date Line.

Since that trip many years ago I have followed the exact same format when planning holidays for friends and now clients within my travel business. The same format applies to each of the many small group tours that I lead around the world. It is simple to follow and can be used for any number of days.

CHAPTER 3

WORKING OUT THE COST AND HOW TO PAY FOR YOUR HOLIDAY

CHAPTER 3

WORKING OUT THE COST AND HOW TO PAY FOR YOUR HOLIDAY

> *Decide you are going to do it. Decide what date you are going to do it by. Write is down and say it out loud. Your dream just became your goal.*

Tarnya Hawkins

Nothing will spoil a holiday more than paying for everything on a credit card and then worrying about how you will pay for it when you get home. Paying for your holiday can actually be easier than you think if you set some simple goals. Saving for something special is a process that your entire family can get involved in. You may want to pay for parts of your holiday on a credit card as there are some benefits to doing this. Some banks offer free travel insurance if you pay more than five hundred dollars of your holiday costs using their particular credit card. Be very sure to read the fine print on these policies though. In fact, be very sure to read the fine print on all travel insurance policies. Many people have had to pay thousands of dollars for things they *thought* were covered on their policies.

You may also want to use your credit card to earn extra points for the loyalty program associated with your card. Using a credit card is fine for either of these examples, just make sure you have the money to pay the cost out in full and not be left with extra interest payments that increase the cost of your holiday.

You do need to do some homework in this chapter to make it all come together and give you a fairly honest idea of what your holiday is going to cost you.

Setup your BUDGET spreadsheet.

Main things to cover are:

- Flights

- Travel Insurance

- Documentation

- Transportation

- Vehicle rental
  * Fuel
  * Parking
  * Tolls

- Accommodation

- Attractions

- Meals
  * Breakfast
  * Lunch
  * Dinner

- Incidentals

- Tipping

- Costs back home while you are away

For most items on the list it was pretty straight forward for us to find out the cost. The big exception was the cost of attractions. The research on this took quite some time as I had to look up each area or place we were visiting and then find out what attractions there were that took our interest. Once I'd made a list, I then had to find out the cost of each attraction and what days and hours the attraction operated to see if it fitted into our schedule.

Set up your ATTRACTIONS spreadsheet.

ATTRACTION	BUDGET	ACTUAL	SURPLUS
Plantation Village			
Dole Plantation Train Tour			
Dole Plantation Garden Tour			
Dole Plantation Maze			
Hanuama Bay Reserve			
Makani Catamaran Cruise			
Kallua Bike Rental			
Iolani Palace			
Hawaii Maritime Centre			
Waikiki Trolley Pass			
Byodo-In Temple			
Outrigger Canoe Surfing			
Pearl Harbour Tour			
Audubon Centre			
Polynesian Cultural Centre			
Sea Kayaking			

ATTRACTION	BUDGET	ACTUAL	SURPLUS
Sea Life Park			
Train to San Francisco			
Alcatraz Island Tour			
Cable Car Rides			
Coit Tower			
Cable Car Barn			
National Maritime Museum			
Aquatic Park			
Cab Fare			
Bus Fare			
National Park Entry Fees			
Monterey Bay Aquarium			
Hearst Castle			
Universal Studios			
Movie Star House Tour			
Hollywood Wax Museum			
Behind the Scenes Tour			
Kodak Theatre Tour			

ATTRACTION	BUDGET	ACTUAL	SURPLUS
Warner Brothers Tour			
Paramount Studios Tour			
Pacific Park Santa Monica			
Bike Rental			
Queen Mary			
Griffith Park Planetarium			
Disneyland			
California Adventure Park			
Knotts Berry Farm			
Mission San Juan Capistrano			
Wild Animal Park			
Seaworld			
San Diego Zoo			
Balboa Park			
San Diego Cruise			
Gondola Ride			
Hoover Dam			
National Park Entry Fees			
Mesa Verde			

ATTRACTION	BUDGET	ACTUAL	SURPLUS
Glenwood Springs			
Sunlight Skiing			
Snow King Skiing			
Ice Hockey Game			
Grand Teton Snowmobiles			
Snowmobile Yellowstone NP			
National Elk Reserve			
Sleigh Ride			
Snowmobiling			
Dog Sleding			
Mt Rushmore			
Crazy Horse Memorial			
Bear Country			
Anheuser-Busch Brewery			
Skyline Drive Fees			
Washington Trolley Tour			
Washington Memorial Tour			
Smithsonian Institute			
Arlington Cemetery			
Arlington House Tour			

ATTRACTION	BUDGET	ACTUAL	SURPLUS
Amish Experience Tour			
Amish Sleigh Ride			
Journey Behind the Falls			
Maid of the Mist			
Seashore Trolley Museum			
Salem Witch Museum			
Boston City Tour			
Boston Harbour Cruise			
Hop On Hop Off Bus			
New York City Sights Tour			
Statue of Liberty			
Ellis Island Ferry			
City Lights Cruise			
Top of the Rock			
Ground Zero Museum			
Ice Skating			
Central Pak Carriage Ride			
Broadway Show			
Off Broadway Show			

ATTRACTION	BUDGET	ACTUAL	SURPLUS
United Nations Building			
Transfer to Airport			
Kennedy Space Centre			
Epcot Centre			
Dolphin Research Centre			
Everglades Tour			
Mississippi River Ferry			
Blaine Keen Mardi Gras World			
Bayou Cruise			
The New Orleans Mint			
Natchez Steamboat Cruise			
Cemetery Tour			
Airport Transfer			
Muir Woods			
Airport Transfer			
Submarine Cruise			
Hawaiian Luau			
Airport Transfer			

This was our budget for three adults for ten weeks. $43,157.00

FLIGHTS			$7,545.00
TRAVEL INSURANCE			$1,126.00
DOCUMENTATION	Visas and 1 Passport		$312.00
TRANSFERS			$200.00
VEHICLE RENTAL			$3,480.00
FUEL			$2,200.00
PARKING			$100.00
TOLLS			$20.00
ACCOMMODATION			$6,900.00
ATTRACTIONS			$9,234.00
MEALS			$8,040.00
INCIDENTALS			$1,000.00
TIPPING			$2,000.00
COSTS BACK HOME			$1,000.00

Once you have worked out your own cost of all of the above items, add these all together. Then work out how much you could put away each week into a high interest account that will penalise you if you take money out. I use an online only high interest account with my bank that allows me to make as many deposits as I like, three withdrawals a month and has no fees or charges.

Let's say your total holiday cost is $30,000 and you could put away $300 per week. Divide the total amount by how much you could put away per week and this will give you how long it will take you to save for your holiday. Without adding any more than $300 you will have $30,000 in 100 weeks, or just less than two years.

Then start putting that money away each week and do not touch it. Treat that payment like a bill that has to be paid each week. You will be surprised at how you can manage without digging into those funds during times when you think there is no other way. Start to find ways to save money.

Let me give you an example of what we did. We had always wanted to have a white Christmas and for years had said, "Hopefully next year we will be able to afford our white Christmas." After saying this for about four years, on that hot January afternoon, we decided we were GOING to have a white Christmas.

I sat down like you are doing now and worked out where we wanted to go, how long we wanted to go for and what we wanted to do when we got there. I did the division and it would take eighty-four weeks of saving $260 per week to take a six week holiday to the United States.

It is also a great idea to give yourself something visual to watch your savings grow. I used a nice hard covered note book and ruled it with four columns. The first column had the date, while the second column had the goal amount I was saving that week. Some weeks we saved more and this extra was added to the third column. The fourth column had our progressive total.

29th April	$260.00		$260.00
6th May	$260.00	$100.00	$620.00
13th May	$260.00	$150.00	$1,030.00
20th May	$260.00	$15.00	$1,305.00
27th May	$260.00		$1,565.00

We started saving and $260 became $620 and then $1,030 and slowly our account was growing. We had set a goal and were on target to fulfil that goal. We could see that this great trip we had dreamed about was going to become a REALITY.

When that happened we really got excited and decided to cut back on a few things so we would have a bit more spending money. We did just a few simple things that really saved us a lot of dollars. The first change was that we took a packed lunch to work each day instead of buying one. The money we saved, about $100 per week, was added to our savings account. We also began to eat our way through the freezer and the pantry, using up all those packets, tins and bottles of stuff that had been sitting there for ages. I must admit we had some interesting meals but we also saved about another $100 per week on groceries until things were pretty bare. All in all, eating like this over a ten week period meant we added another $1,500 to our account. We looked for other ways to save as well, not going out so often, using just one car instead of two if we were going in the same direction. Very soon we were actually saving $400 per week instead of our original goal of $260 per week.

One year later at week fifty-two we had saved $17,490.

By now we had pretty much tied down the departure date, so we kept on track with our eighty-four week savings plan. What we were able to do though was to start adding extra days and then weeks to our holiday. We both work for ourselves so we decided that if we could get someone to look after our business, we could actually have a longer holiday. They say that when you set actual goals, unexplained things begin to happen. It seems the whole universe is on your side helping you reach those goals.

Suddenly a friend was available to look after our business and what went from being a six week holiday to experience a white Christmas became the ten week holiday of a lifetime.

There are other things to take into consideration such as who will look after things while you are gone, including your children if you are planning a child free get away.

> *Regardless of where you are going for your holiday or break or how you plan on travelling, there are special deals happening all the time.*

As I mentioned earlier, flights can be cheaper on certain days of the week while flights on a weekend are the most expensive. So keep an eye on that and look for deals. Regardless of where you are going for your holiday or break or how you plan on travelling, there are special deals happening all the time.

You will also need to keep an eye on the currency fluctuations of the country you are visiting. When we started planning our holiday the Australian dollar was buying about seventy-five cents American. By the time we went on holidays it was closer to eighty-five cents, so we gained some extra dollars there as well. On one particular trip to the United States when I was in my twenties the Australian dollar dropped without me realising this. I thought one Australian dollar was buying seventy-five American cents, when in actual fact it was only buying sixty American cents.

Currency fluctuations were not even something I was aware of back then, until my credit card had run out of money while I was in New Orleans towards the end of my holiday. My flights to get back home to Australia were paid for but I didn't have money for anything else, including food. I spent three days eating the broken fortune cookies that they give away for free in San Francisco, and doing a lot of walking until it was time for me to fly home.

Ever since that holiday, I now carry a preloaded currency card and each night before I go to bed, I write down what I have spent that day. Make sure you always get a receipt every time you purchase something and have these to fall back on each night to jog your memory. As well as carrying a preloaded currency card, it is always a good idea to have some cash for the country you are visiting as you do not want to be exchanging money at any airport, where the exchange rates are terrible. I personally use Kings or Crown Currency as they are an Australian owned company and give the best rates and service I have encountered so far, with no fees or commissions.

You can find them at www.crowncurrency.com.au

When I do my ATTRACTIONS spreadsheet, I add in all the attractions we might like to go to or see with the advertised cost. When you get to the attraction, sometimes the price may be cheaper than what was advertised. This is where I put in the actual cost. The difference in price is put in the surplus column. On other occasions, things will happen and you won't get to a particular attraction on your list. When this happens, put what you would have spent in the surplus column. The amount in this column will become your little backup plan if you want to go somewhere else that was not budgeted for. There were many things on our attraction list that we did not get around to doing and we were able to use this surplus money for other activities we discovered during our holiday. While we had a tour through the Everglades down on our schedule, it was a secret wish of mine to actually drive one of the airboats that they use. With some of our surplus money we were able to charter our own private airboat and I got to experience driving one under the watchful eye of the airboat captain.

CHAPTER 4

WHO WILL LOOK AFTER EVERYTHING AT HOME WHILE I'M AWAY?

CHAPTER 4

WHO WILL LOOK AFTER EVERYTHING AT HOME WHILE I'M AWAY?

> 66 *What you've done becomes the judge of what you're going to do — especially in other people's minds. When you're travelling, you are what you are right there and then. People don't have your past to hold against you. No yesterdays on the road.* 99

William Least Heat Moon

Who would look after our business while we were away was perhaps our biggest concern but there were certainly other facts of life that would need to be taken care of as well. To start with, we had two small dogs that we did not want to leave in a boarding kennel for that length of time. We wanted to find a house sitter who would look after things like the animals, plants and security while we were away.

We wrote down a list of things that would need to be addressed so we could go away knowing that everything would be taken care of at home and we could just concentrate on having a good time. We did not feel the need to call home to check on anything while we were away.

Print your AWAY FROM HOME CHECKLIST from
www.travellingmadeeasy.com.au

	CHECKLIST
✔	**WHO WILL LOOK AFTER WHERE I LIVE?**
	What will they do in an emergency?
	Will I lock up or get a house sitter?
	Who will collect mail?
	Do I need extra home security?
	Who will put the rubbish out for collection the first week I'm away?
	Who will water the plants?
	Who will mow the lawns?
✔	**WHO WILL LOOK AFTER PETS?**
	How much food do I need to buy for my pets while I'm away?
	What is the feeding schedule for my pets?
	What are the veterinary details for my pets?
	Who will I leave insurance details with?

✔	**WHO WILL LOOK AFTER MY CHILDREN?**
	Who will take them to school and school activities?
	What is the medical information for my children including optometrist and dentist?
	What are the health insurance details for my children?
	What is the list of rules and behaviour expected from my children?
	How are my children disciplined?
✔	**WHO WILL LOOK AFTER MY JOB?**
	What do I need to put in place to make it as easy as possible for this person to do my job while I am away?
	Who should they contact if they need help with any part of my job that they don't understand?
✔	**WHO WILL LOOK AFTER ELDERLY RELATIVES?**
	What is the medical stuff that relates to my elderly relatives... so they know what to look for?

As we were going to be away for ten weeks and were still operating our business while we were gone, we wanted to make sure our friend left running the business would be able to access accounts if necessary. We were able to set up an account that she could access and got her a work credit card.

For us, it was in our best interests to have a power of attorney. You need to be extremely wise in this choice as you are giving this person a lot of power. We only chose one; a very trusted dear friend. If in doubt, choose two people who are not related and stipulate that all decisions have to be made together.

We had ticked off our entire checklist covering every possible scenario while we were away. It was time to start looking at what documents and vaccinations we might need.

CHAPTER 5

TRAVEL DOCUMENTS AND VACCINATIONS

CHAPTER 5

TRAVEL DOCUMENTS AND VACCINATIONS

> *It's great to take a few risks in life but in some situations you need to cover all the bases.*

Tarnya Hawkins

The first of course is a valid passport for each person who is travelling overseas. For most countries you are required to have six months validity left on your passport when you return home. If you need to apply for a new passport or a replacement passport, the procedure is fairly simple if you follow these easy steps. If you are applying for an Australian passport or wish to renew a current Australian passport go to www.passports.gov.au.

> *For most countries you are required to have six months validity left on your passport when you return home.*

If you are applying for a New Zealand passport or wish to renew a current New Zealand passport go to www.passports.govt.nz.

If you are applying for an American passport or wish to renew an American passport go to www.travel.state.gov.

If you are applying for a British passport or wish to renew a British passport go to www.gov.uk.

You will then need to decide if you need a visa to visit the country you are travelling to or for any stopovers made on the way. The easiest way to do this is by going to www.visahq.com.au.

Since 2003 VisaHQ.com, Inc. has provided online visa services and U.S. passport solutions enabling travellers to apply online for visas to virtually any country in the world. Using unmatched, cutting-edge online technologies, customers can apply for travel visas simply by filling out one universal, 100% paperless electronic form. They can also obtain, renew, replace or add pages to passports for U.S. citizens.

Some countries require that you have vaccinations before you can visit and you must show proof of having had these done. For other countries, it may not be a requirement but it would be in your best interests to take precautions.

For information on which vaccinations you may need for the countries you are travelling to, go to www.health.gov.au or going to the travel section of www.vaccinehub.com.au provides an interactive world map. Simply choose which countries you will be visiting and they will list the recommended vaccinations for that particular country.

You will require inoculations and certificates of such for yellow fever if you are travelling through some African and South American countries. You need to be aware and take precautions against mosquito bites in the Caribbean, Central and South America and Africa. For more information on yellow fever go to www.yellowfever.com.au

Yellow fever is a viral disease that is transmitted primarily by mosquitoes. Yellow fever can lead to serious illness and even death. It is called 'yellow fever' because, in serious cases, the skin turns yellow in colour. This is known as 'jaundice.' Yellow fever is a quarantinable disease in Australia and most western countries.

Australia's list of yellow fever declared places includes forty-three countries. The list is guided by World Health Organisation's list of yellow fever endemic countries and also takes into account recent international surveillance data.

Africa

- Angola
- Benin
- Burkina Faso
- Burundi
- Cameroon
- Central African Republic
- Chad
- Congo, Democratic Republic of the
- Congo, Republic of the
- Cote d'Ivoire (Ivory Coast)
- Equatorial Guinea
- Ethiopia
- Gabon
- Gambia
- Ghana
- Guinea
- Guinea-Bissau
- Kenya
- Liberia
- Mali
- Mauritania
- Niger

- Nigeria
- Rwanda
- Senegal
- Sierra Leone
- South Sudan
- Sudan
- Togo
- Uganda

South America & Central America

- Argentina – Misiones Province
- Bolivia
- Brazil
- Colombia
- Ecuador excluding Galapagos Islands
- French Guiana
- Guyana
- Panama
- Paraguay
- Peru
- Suriname
- Trinidad
- Venezuela

My advice is that you should always see your doctor before you travel, to firstly get a check up and clear bill of health and secondly to discuss what vaccinations you need and tablets to carry. It is always a good idea, regardless of what country you are travelling to, to have a letter from your doctor outlining any medication that you take and if there are any other problems associated with your health. This could be as simple as a knee replacement or the more complicated fact that you need to carry an oxygen bottle.

Documentation from a doctor will go a long way if you find yourself with a health problem in a foreign county. It is always a good idea to make sure all your medications from a chemist or pharmacy are labelled correctly and that these labels have your name clearly printed on them.

Mosquitoes are public enemy number one. They are carriers of some of the world's most deadly diseases, including malaria which kills more than a million people annually. Be sure to take necessary travel vaccination precautions, see your doctor about anti-malaria medications, pack insect repellent and wear light clothes that cover your arms and legs at dusk to avoid the risk of infection.

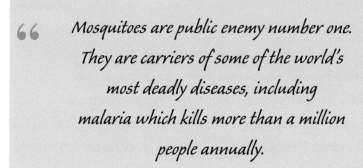

> *Mosquitoes are public enemy number one. They are carriers of some of the world's most deadly diseases, including malaria which kills more than a million people annually.*

Safe drinking water is something we just take for granted in Australia but forty percent of the world's population does not have access to clean drinking water and adequate sanitation facilities. Always buy sealed bottled water when travelling in areas with unsafe drinking water, avoid any drinks that have ice in them and don't use tap water to brush your teeth. I would also recommend only eating food that has been cooked by some type of high heat. Be aware that salad vegetables may have been washed in unsafe drinking water. I learnt this lesson the hard way on one particularly memorable trip to South America.

Keep all your documents in a safe place and have photocopies stored somewhere that you can easily access if you need to.

CHECKLIST	
Passport	
Visas	
Flight Tickets	
Train Tickets	
Bus Tickets	
Cruise Vouchers	
Accommodation Vouchers	
Tour Vouchers	
Itinerary	
Reservations	
Travel Insurance Details	
Health Insurance Details	
Drivers Licence	
International Drivers Licence	
SCUBA Licence	
Boat Licence	
Student ID Card	
Youth Hostel Card	
Senior Citizen Card	
Vaccination Card	
Passport Photos	

	Contact Information	
	Allergy Card	
	Business Cards	
	Credit Cards	
	Multi Currency Cash Card	
	Debit Card	
	Cash	
	Cash [Foreign]	
	Phone Card	

CHAPTER 6

WILL I LIKE THE FOOD?

CHAPTER 6

WILL I LIKE THE FOOD?

> 66 *If you reject the food, ignore the customs,*
> *fear the religion and avoid the people, you*
> *might better stay at home.* 99

James Michener

Being such a foodie and having experienced American food before, I wanted to make sure my travelling companions got to try as many different styles of American cuisine as possible. Because people from so many different nations worldwide now call America home, this was going to be research I knew I would enjoy. I thought back to the many new experiences I had had with food in the past as I travelled throughout the world.

One of the joys of travelling is experiencing new foods, new ways of eating new foods and new times for eating familiar foods. For example, we would not consider eating spicy pork, prawns or rice for breakfast and yet this is as common in some Asian countries as our bowl of cereal and piece of toast.

Porridge may seem like an ordinary breakfast food unless you are in Thailand where it is known as congee and is made from short grain rice which is boiled in a chicken, beef or pork stock until it is very thick. You then have a multitude of different toppings and garnishes such as pork pieces, chicken pieces, crab, prawns, eggs, spring onion, ginger, sprouts or anything else that takes your fancy. While it is traditionally a breakfast dish it is served all day in street markets.

If you are travelling through South America and particularly Columbia, you will encounter a breakfast favourite called calentado. This meal is usually made from leftovers, such as rice, beans, potatoes and plantain, from the evening meal the night before and which are reheated. You may also find on your breakfast plate, chorizo, different types of grilled meat, sautéed onions, tomatoes and fried eggs. Cornflour cakes known as arepas are also popular in Columbia and are served with most meals. These can be served plain where you might add some butter or they can be filled with cheese. In Columbia you will be offered a hot chocolate drink called chocolate caliente colombiano which is served with coconut milk and is quite delicious.

If visiting Hong Kong, join the locals first thing in the morning at little cafes called cha chaan teng, for breakfast. You will experience authentic local cuisine at authentic local prices. You may not think about this as a breakfast food but the most popular is the fish ball noodle soup. These hearty bowls full of vermicelli, also known as rice noodles, fish balls and vegetables will give you a warm and filling start to your day.

In the United Kingdom you are more likely to find what is known as a full breakfast or also referred to as an English breakfast or fry up. Reflecting the location where you are eating, it may also be known as full Scottish, full Welsh, full Irish or Ulster fry. The items served for breakfast will depend on the area but all are usually served with staples of sausage, bacon, poached or fried eggs, grilled tomato, fried mushrooms, baked beans, toast and a mug of tea. Sometimes black pudding is added and also a dish known as bubble and squeak which is made from left over mashed potatoes and cabbage, mixed together with butter and then fried. In England, a full breakfast is also known as a full Monty.

In Cornwall you might also get Cornish potato cakes, made with mashed potatoes mixed with butter and flour and then fried or gurty pudding, a Cornish dish similar to haggis. Don't confuse this with gurty milk, another Cornish breakfast dish made with bread and milk. Traditional Cornish breakfasts might also include pilchards and herring.

In Ireland you are likely to have added to the usual bacon and eggs, such things as fried liver and brown soda bread. If soda bread isn't served, you may be offered an alternative such as potato farl, boxy or toast. The breakfast roll, a baguette style bread filled with things such as bacon, eggs, cheese and sausages, has become very popular as it is easy to eat on the way to school or work. It is available at most convenience stores and fuel stations right across Ireland.

In Scotland, be sure to try the Scottish style black pudding, haggis, white pudding, fruit pudding and oatcakes. Porridge is also popular in Scotland and is usually served as a starter. My favourite is the tattie scones made from you guessed it....potatoes and lorne sausage.

When eating breakfast in Wales, make sure you taste laver bread which is a seaweed puree mixed with oatmeal and then fried. This is served with bacon, eggs and cockles.

In Jamaica, fruits such as papaya, passionfruit, mango, and pineapple make up a big part of the breakfast menu. They also have a dish called ackee which looks like scrambled eggs but is made from fruit of the lychee family, breadfruit and plantains. Most breakfast meals include some type of salted fish, usually cod.

A breakfast in Turkey will be set out like a huge buffet and everyone sits together to enjoy the communal experience. You will find choices of cold meats, olives, tomatoes in olive oil, cheese, which is creamy and slightly salty and similar to a fetta, the spicy cheese known as Kelek, homemade fruit preserves, bagels and sourdough bread. Turkish menemen which consists of chopped onions, peppers, tomato, garlic and eggs is also served. Strong black brewed tea is served with sugar.

I knew we would enjoy breakfast in America. The choices are endless. Eggs that are fried, poached, boiled, scrambled or cooked in an omelet. Denver omelettes that are multi layered. Meats such as bacon, ham, sausage, corned beef hash, link sausages, spam, steak or country fried steak. Potatoes done as hash browns, fried potatoes or home fries. Toast choices such as white, wheat, rye, sourdough or English muffins, bagels, waffles, pancakes, cinnamon rolls, biscuits, gravy. Throw into the choices muesli, oatmeal, grits or an abundance of cold cereals and a multitude of different fruit juices or milks.

As our first stop would be Hawaii, I searched the internet for local restaurants and cafes where we could try some of the local cuisine such as poi, made from the taro root and laulau which is made from the taro leaves. We would get to try kalua pig which is slow cooked in an underground oven known as an imu and poke, the Hawaiian version of Japanese sashimi. While poke uses tuna, tako is made using octopus and both have a splash of soy sauce, Hawaiian sea salt, sweet onions and limu which is a type of seaweed plant. Lomi-lomi salmon is a salsa of raw salmon cured with salt, diced tomatoes, onions and chilli peppers. While spam is an all-time favourite in Hawaii, with even a festival in its honour, it was not on our list of must try foods.

We would be visiting Fisherman's Wharf in San Francisco where you really must eat clam chowder from a sourdough roll. We would also be visiting the region known as New England which has a long history of culture and cuisine from the first pilgrims who landed at Plymouth Rock to the thriving lobster and maple syrup production of today. It has some of the best seafood and dairy products in the country and this combination makes for some amazing chowder. There are four main types of chowder with the most popular being the cream based clam chowder followed by the Manhattan clam chowder, a tomato based clam soup which was adapted by the Portuguese immigrants who settled in the Rhode Island area and whose home country cuisine influenced their cooking. Rhode Island also has a version of clam chowder that uses a clear broth and the state's signature quahogs, a type of hard clam that is found in abundance in this area. Last but not least is the New Hampshire twist on chowder, using bacon and corn instead of clams. Clams can also be prepared in a variety of ways, from raw to fried and clam bakes are common in this part of the world.

Maine is the largest producer of lobster in the nation and it is served in just about every way imaginable. The most popular is the lobster roll, a hotdog bun filled with cooked chilled lobster meat mixed with mayonnaise. My favourite is still a freshly steamed lobster served with drawn butter.

Vermont is the biggest producer of maple syrup in the United States although Quebec in Canada holds the record for largest worldwide production. Perhaps this is the reason that baked beans, a dish that originated in New England, is sweetened with maple syrup in Maine and further north, while down in Boston they are sweetened with molasses and called Boston beans.

> 66 *Vermont is the biggest producer of maple syrup in the United States although Quebec in Canada holds the record for largest worldwide production.* 99

Because the early settlers found wheat impossible to grow, a cornmeal griddle cake, called a Johnny cake, was created. You will be served these as a side in all New England restaurants. Vermont is also home to the world famous Ben & Jerry's Ice Cream. A company started by two friends in 1978 which has now grown to an international product in over thirty countries. It seems as if they create new flavours every week but my favourite is still chunky monkey and as the name suggests, has chunks of chocolate in a banana ice cream. I love banana splits and I always have one when I am near a Ben & Jerry's.

> *A proper Pennsylvania Dutch meal supposedly consists of seven sweets and seven sours.*

I was also looking forward to visiting the Amish area of Pennsylvania where the origins are actually German, not Dutch. The great myth is that Pennsylvania Dutch means Amish, when in fact the Amish represent only about 5 percent of the total Pennsylvania Dutch population. Like other regional fare, Pennsylvania Dutch foods come with their own unique lingo: Lebanon bologna, schnitz, knepp, scrapple and shoofly pies. A proper Pennsylvania Dutch meal supposedly consists of seven sweets and seven sours. I never remembered to count them as I was always too busy eating. I think the best part of this style of cooking is that it is all hand made from scratch and makes you feel like you are eating at your grandmother's house. The humble hot dog also has German origins.

New Orleans was on our list of places to visit. We were looking forward to listening to some great jazz music and taking a paddleboat ride on the Mississippi. We were also pretty excited about trying Creole and Cajun food but what exactly was the difference.

The really simple answer is that Creole cuisine uses tomatoes and Cajun food does not. So if we were eating a gumbo or jambalaya that had a tomato base, we would know this was Creole food. If you talk to someone from Louisiana they will tell you that Creole food comes from the city, namely New Orleans, while Cajun food comes from the country areas and the bayous.

Having spent time in the south of America on previous trips, I was looking forward to enjoying soul food, which is a variety of cuisine popular in the African American culture. The name, soul food became popular in the 1960s but the origins go way back in history. Rice, sorghum and okra, which are all common elements in West African cooking, were introduced to America during the time of the trans Atlantic slave trade. Other foods such as corn and cassava from Central America, turnips from Morocco and cabbage from Portugal would play an important role in the history of African American cooking.

Slaves were fed the leftovers from the plantation houses and were soon cooking with new types of green vegetables such as the tops of turnips, beets, collards, kale, cress and pokeweed.

It is interesting to note that many of the soul food dishes eaten by the early slaves and still eaten by southerners today were and are also eaten by the Native Americans in the south western United States. Foods such as cornbread and boiled cornbread, which is also called cornmeal dumplings or hushpuppies, are a staple. Sofkee is still eaten but is now called grits, and beans, peas and greens are boiled. Southerners still cure their meat and smoke it over hickory coals just as the Native Americans do. Today the meal is a little different but the basics are the same. A traditional soul food dinner will consist of fried chicken or catfish, collard greens, breaded fried okra, mashed potatoes and cornbread.

With Mexico just over the border the influence of Mexican food in the United States is very strong. Original Mexican food was a combination of corn, beans, chilli peppers and small amounts of wild meat. After the Spanish conquest of the Aztec Empire in the 16th century, other foods were introduced. These included meats such as pork, beef, chicken and lamb, cheese and lots of different spices. The Mexican food we eat today has evolved into something quite different from those early dishes and to a degree, what you will find in authentic Mexican restaurants anywhere in Central America. In the south east of America in particular, you do come pretty close to eating authentic Mexican cuisine with dishes like barbacoa, mole poblano, cochinitapibil, menudo, molotes, sopes and tacos made with carnitas filling. While I haven't seen the extremely popular toasted grasshoppers anywhere in the United States I have eaten them while travelling in Mexico. In Texas they have what is called the TexMex fusion and in southern California it is CalMex. I could already picture myself enjoying a plate full of flautas with guacamole and drinking my favourite lemon margarita from a salt rimmed glass.

Texas is home to some of the most amazing steaks I have ever eaten and if you are really up to the challenge, there is a place in Amarillo called the Big Texan Steak Ranch where you can attempt to eat a seventy-two ounce steak with sides in under an hour, and if you do, your meal is free. On the 26th of May, 2014 the one hundred and twenty-five pound competitive eater, Molly Schuyler, polished off the meal in just four minutes and fifty-eight seconds and came back for seconds finishing both meals in fourteen minutes and fifty-seven seconds.

Each place we had down to visit seemed to have a food speciality of its own whether that was Jewish in New York City, Danish in Solvang or Cuban at Key West. I even went as far as writing out a list because I knew I wouldn't remember it all. The list was just to act as a guide of what to look out for as we travelled around. The list looked something like this.

PLACE	AREA FOOD SPECIALITIES
Honolulu	Hawaiian Poi, Laulau, Lomi-lomi, Kalua Pig, Poke, Polynesian Luau, Pineapple, Papaya, Coffee, Bubbies Ice Cream Balls
San Francisco	Chinese Dim Sum and Fortune Cookies, Clam Chowder in a Sour Dough Bowl, Ghirardelli Chocolate, Soft Pretzels
Santa Cruz	Caramel Apples
Morro Bay	Freshly caught Seafood
Solvang	Danish Pastries
Los Angeles	Diddie Reese Ice Cream Cookies, In-N-Out Burger
Disneyland	Corn Dogs
San Juan Capistrano	Rolled Tacos
San Diego	Mexican
Las Vegas	Hash House A Go Go
Route 66	A Hoagie
Jackson, Wyoming	Cowboy Steaks and Ribs
Omaha	Steaks
Kansas	Bar-B-Q
Louisville	Soul Food
Kentucky	Chilli and Cornbread, Fried Green Tomatoes, Hushpuppies, Grits

PLACE	AREA FOOD SPECIALITIES
Washington DC	Pizza, Pecan Pie
Lancaster County	Amish Style Cooking, Shoofly Pie, Red Velvet Cake
Niagara Falls	Pancakes and Maple Syrup, Canadian Bacon, Buffalo Wings
Vermont	Ben & Jerry's Ice Cream, Maple Syrup
Maine	Lobster, Johnny Cakes, New England Clam Chowder
Boston	Indian Food, Boston Beans
New York	Smoked Salmon and Cream Cheese Bagels, Deep Dish Pizza, Martini
Florida	Soft Shell Crabs
Key West	Fresh Seafood
New Orleans	Muffaletta Sandwich, Crawfish Étouffée, Gumbo, Jambalaya, Poboys, Beignets at Cafe Du Monde, Dirty Rice, Red Beans, Creole Shrimp, Aunt Sally's Pralines

There is so much to say about the great variety of cuisine you can find and sample in the United States but that might have to wait for another book. There is so much more to America than hot dogs, hamburgers and pizza. You will find the best breakfast at a little place in Lebanon, Missouri called Miss Mary's Lunch Box, or Corky's in San Bernadino, California. Be adventurous and try as many new and different foods as you possibly can, wherever you travel in the world.

CHAPTER 7

WHAT AM I GOING TO EAT? FOOD ALLERGIES AND DIETS

"Oh, it's alright. You couldn't know that I'm honey-intolerant."

CHAPTER 7

WHAT AM I GOING TO EAT?
FOOD ALLERGIES AND DIETS

> 66 *Eating different foods is one of the great pleasures of travelling. Some research before you go will help, as will a language translator App or device. With the variety of food available in most destinations, there will always be something for the most careful of eaters.* 99

Di Hillman

If you have food allergies or follow a particular diet when you are home, you may be fearful of travelling, especially to overseas countries or places where you cannot speak the local language. Even if you can speak the language, sometimes specific ingredients can be hidden in food without you actually knowing unless you read the fine print on the ingredient list. This is particularly true for anyone with coeliac [also known as celiac] disease or gluten intolerance.

Refusing to let their diet be an obstacle to enjoying all that travel has to offer, people with specific food allergies or diets can have a fabulous time and try lots of new taste sensations. You do need to take a little longer doing some careful planning and be willing to communicate your needs very clearly. Sometimes you need to repeat your requests several times before your waiter gets what you mean and what you are asking for. One instance that springs to mind is of a particular waiter who couldn't understand why a vegetable soup wasn't vegetarian just because it was cooked in chicken stock.

Do some research on the areas in the world you will be visiting so you will be prepared for some of the challenges you may face when you get there. India, for example, has nearly one third of their entire population who are vegetarian, so you will find lots of meatless dishes to choose from. Lots of Indian dishes are thickened with nuts, especially cashews, so if you are nut intolerant this will be a problem you will need to look out for. In South America, your waiters will have no clue what you are talking about when it comes to being a vegetarian or vegan as this is a foreign concept to them. It may take you a while longer but with clear explanations that you sometimes have to repeat a number of times, you can eat your way through a variety of South American meals and fiestas.

One of the easiest ways to get your point across, particularly if you are in a country where you don't speak the local language, is to use food allergy translation cards. Some of these cards explain your allergy or dietary restriction translated into different languages and you can choose which language you want to buy your set in, while others have photos of the foods you can't eat. You can also get food allergy translation cards that are custom made just for your specific allergies. These are particularly helpful if you have allergies to more than just one food group. These cards are usually wallet sized so very easy to carry with you. It is also a good idea to order a couple of sets in case you lose them or forget to get them back from the waiter. It's a simple idea that could literally save your life if your allergy is life threatening. There are a number of companies that offer food allergy translation cards and you can find them on the internet. Some I know of are Allergy Translation, SelectWisely and Dietary Card. The International Vegetarian Union has a directory of vegetarian phrases in a variety of different languages while www.CeliacTravel.com has printable gluten free cards in forty-two different languages.

If at all possible, check the internet for restaurants near where you will be staying that can accommodate your food choices. Typing into an internet search engine something as simple as "gluten free restaurants in Sydney" or wherever you are visiting, will normally bring up a selection for you to look at and you will be able to find one or two that are close to where you will be. Some of the sites offer reviews from people who have eaten there and give other information like expected costs, wait times, if the staff are friendly and accommodating and if there is nearby parking. If I know I have passengers on my tours with specific food allergies I will always do this and if necessary, even ring the restaurant and talk with the chef before I arrive. Sometimes I get caught out when I arrive and the menu or staff has changed and what was on the original menu is no longer an option.

Wherever you are eating, once you arrive at the restaurant or cafe, address your dietary needs with your waiter or if possible, the chef. The chef may be the only person who knows the exact ingredients for each particular dish on the menu. Show your food allergy cards if you have them and don't be afraid to ask the chef to modify a dish or prepare something that isn't necessarily on the menu. This will be a lot easier for the kitchen staff to do if you are eating before or after the busiest peak time. If you are eating at a chain restaurant and you find a number of things you can eat on the menu, then chances are that you can eat these same things in each of their restaurants. P F Chang's Chinese Restaurant Chain across the United States, for example, has a great gluten free and vegetarian menu.

Also be sure to look up websites that offer information for your particular food allergy and see what resources they have available for travellers.

Springing up now are different tour companies that cater for specific diets and this will take all the hard work and hassle out of where and what to eat. You can take a kosher cruise with Kosherica or experience a vegetarian biking trip throughout England with a company called Bicycle Beano.

The safest way to control what you eat if you have very life threatening allergies is to book accommodation that has a kitchen or where you can cook for yourself. You can find many hotels that have suites that come with a kitchen or another alternative is to do a house exchange. You can then purchase fresh food from a local grocery store, food market or health food store and prepare this the way you like to eat it. Another option could be staying at bed and breakfast establishments, especially if you can negotiate with the owners to be allowed access to their kitchen.

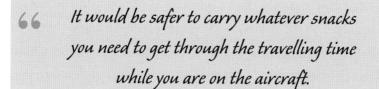

> *It would be safer to carry whatever snacks you need to get through the travelling time while you are on the aircraft.*

Let's talk a little bit about travelling by plane. These days, domestic airlines in most countries no longer offer complimentary in-flight meals but rather have a number of snacks available for purchase. Very few offer anything substantial for those with a special diet. It would be safer to carry whatever snacks you need to get through the travelling time while you are on the aircraft. Be aware of carrying excess food that may not be permitted into the area or country you are flying to. If in doubt, leave it on the aircraft.

Most long haul international flights do offer in-flight meals and just about every airline will accommodate a variety of special diets as long as they have enough notice. You need to request a special meal when you book your ticket and confirm with the airline at least twenty-four hours in advance of your departure time. Be sure to mention your special diet request when you check in to make certain this information is in the system. Usually, but not always, there is a note printed on your boarding pass saying that you require a special meal. Once you are on board the aircraft you should inform the flight attendant that you have requested a special meal. This is particularly important if your seat reservation has changed before your flight.

If, for some reason, you need to change the airline that you originally booked with, be sure to ring them and let them know about your special meal request as this information may not automatically be sent to the new carrier. If you miss a connecting flight and you are put on a later flight you will also need to let the airline know of your special meal request. In most cases they will do all they can to make sure you have something to eat on board even though this cannot be guaranteed as your original request would have been loaded onto the flight you missed. Always carry some snacks with you and that you can eat on the plane if something goes wrong and your special request meal doesn't arrive.

Again, be aware of quarantine laws about taking specific foods into some countries if you have anything left over.

At the moment, Virgin International flights offer the following special meals and require forty-eight hours notice. Most other international airlines offer a similar selection.

Asian Vegetarian Meal - A vegetarian meal and is likely to be spicy in nature.
Currently available on all flights.

Baby Meal - A meal only suitable for those under eighteen months of age.
Currently available on all flights.

Child Meal - Only available for passengers under the age of twelve.
Currently available on all flights.

Diabetic Meal - A meal low in fat and sugar but high in fibre.
Currently available on all flights.

Gluten Free Meal - Contains no foods with barley, wheat, rye or oats and milk and milk products are avoided where possible. Suitable for passengers with coeliac disease.

Currently available on all flights.

Hindu Meal - Contains no pork, beef or veal or products containing these meats. This meal is non vegetarian and likely to be spicy in nature.

Currently available on all flights.

Jain Meal - A strict vegan meal containing no root vegetables.

Currently available on all flights.

Kosher Meal - All kosher foods provided are prepared and served in accordance with the strict Jewish dietary requirements.

Currently unavailable on flights departing from Delhi, Havana, Lagos and all Caribbean destinations.

Low Fat Meal - This meal will be prepared using low fat cooking methods and contains high fibre content and minimum levels of additional fats.

Currently available on all flights.

Low Salt Meal - No further salt will be added to the products used during the cooking process of these dishes.

Currently available on all flights.

Muslim Meal - These meals contain no pork or alcohol or derivatives of these products.

Currently available on all flights.

Vegan Meal - Contains no meat, meat products, fish, fowl, eggs or dairy products.

Currently available on all flights.

Vegetarian Lactose Meal - These meals contain no meat, meat products, fish or fowl but may contain dairy products as well as eggs. Any cheeses contained within these meals are vegetarian based.

Currently available on all flights.

Special Requirements Meal - Any specific and essential dietary requirements not met by the meals above can be ordered through the airlines Special Assistance Department.

Currently available on all flights.

Different international airlines offer different selections so it would be wise to visit their website and see what is available before booking your ticket.

For travellers who are sensitive to peanuts, any travel including travelling on an aircraft can be a source of worry and concern. Firstly, check the website of the airline you wish to travel with to determine their policy on any foods containing nuts. Very few airlines now serve peanuts on flights, while others refrain from serving them if they know they have a passenger on board who has a severe allergy. No airline can guarantee a peanut free aircraft because they have no control over what passengers may carry on board. However, you can take some control over your situation by explaining to other passengers near you that you have a severe peanut allergy and also by asking the flight attendant to make an announcement over the PA system on your behalf. Take some sanitary wipes with you when travelling and wipe down your armrests and tray table before eating. You might also consider taking early morning nonstop flights as the aircraft will be at its cleanest then.

Ask your doctor to write a letter explaining your medical condition, your medical history and how you should be treated should you have a severe allergic reaction. Ask them to include their contact details in case someone needs to speak with them. If you are travelling to a country or countries that do not speak English, have this letter translated into the local language or languages. It may seem like a lot of work before you go but peace of mind is a wonderful thing while travelling. Carry this letter with you in your purse or wallet at all times. It might be in your best interests to also wear a medic alert bracelet. Carry enough antihistamines, epinephrine needles and any other medication you need to deal with your allergic reactions, so that they will last for the entire trip and a few days afterwards on the off-chance that your travel arrangements are delayed. Always carry these items in your carry-on luggage so that they are easy to get to and you won't be without them if your checked baggage gets lost. You will need to show these items to security officers particularly if you are flying and while you will be allowed to carry these items on board, additional screening may be required, so give yourself a little extra time to allow for this.

If you do need to carry an EpiPen with you, make sure your travelling companion knows where it is kept, how to use it and is able to administer the dose required for your allergic reaction if you are unable to do so.

An additional precaution would be to research hospitals and doctors or other medical providers wherever you are going, particularly if the reaction to certain foods is life threatening. Make sure that whatever travel insurance you use will cover allergies as a pre-existing medical condition and will cover any medical expenses you might incur if you have an allergic reaction requiring medical attention. Make sure you read the fine print and ask as many questions as possible to make sure you have everything covered. Medical expenses while travelling overseas can amount to thousands of dollars.

For more personal research go to: www.wanderlust.co.uk for an Anaphylaxis Air Travel Checklist.

Most cruise ship lines will look after your dietary requirements as long as you give them enough notice. Have your travel agent put in a request for your special meals when they book your ticket or if you are doing the booking yourself, make sure you put this information in the comments section. Once on board, let your steward know as soon as possible about your dietary requirements. Vegetarians will find at least one choice in most restaurants or in the buffet section of the ship, while other diets may have to be ordered in advance.

CHAPTER 8

WHAT SHOULD I PACK?

CHAPTER 8

WHAT SHOULD I PACK?

> " *The lighter you travel, the more you will enjoy the journey.* "

Tarnya Hawkins

As you are planning your holiday you will need to ask yourself a number of questions and this will determine how much or how little you decide to pack. Be brutally honest with your answers. The first question should always be, 'How strong is my back?' If you suffer from any back problems, you do not want to be using a backpack. If your back is strong, a rolling backpack is a great way to go. A rolling backpack can be worn on your back but also has wheels and a pull out handle for when you want to just drag it along.

The trick is always to have a backpack or carry-on suitcase small enough to stow in an overhead aircraft storage bin or under the seat in front of you in a train or bus. The more you travel, the lighter you will travel. I've yet to meet someone who says, 'The more I travel, the more luggage I take with me.'

You should *never* travel with more than one suitcase. Too much luggage will mark you as a tourist and tourists are an easy target for those who make a living from conning others. With only one bag you are in control and much more able to move around quickly if need be. Take this advice very seriously.

> 66
>
> *You should never travel with more than one suitcase.*
>
> 99

You will have to walk with your luggage more than you realise. Even if you are on a tour that delivers your baggage to your room, you will still need to carry your luggage whenever you are using public transport. Airports and train stations can be massive in some cities. Take your luggage for a quick test run *before* you leave home. Pack everything you are planning on taking into your bag and then take it into your local town or city and walk around with it for about an hour. Fully loaded, this should be an enjoyable walk. If it isn't, then head home and revisit your packing list.

This exercise also gives you an indication of the condition of your bag. If you are using a suitcase with wheels, do all the wheels work correctly and roll smoothly? Do the zippers work properly? Does the handle pull out and retract easily? If using a backpack, are the straps all in good condition and are they comfortable?

Check with the airline you are travelling with to determine their baggage policies and weight limits before you start to pack and make sure you weigh your bag before you leave home so you don't get a nasty surprise at check in. Airlines will not allow bags to be overweight anymore and they will ask you to remove items or charge hefty fees, sometimes in the hundreds of dollars. The weight limit for checked baggage for most airlines is twenty kilograms or fifty pounds.

Wherever possible, take nothing more than carry-on luggage with you. Make sure you stay within the carry-on luggage limit of fifty-five centimetres by thirty-five centimetres by twenty-three centimetres or twenty two inches by fourteen inches by nine inches. Make sure your bag does not weigh more than seven kilograms or fifteen pounds. You will also need to check on the latest airport security restrictions at each of the airports you are travelling from. Take particular notice of any liquids you are carrying as new rules have been applied to protect you from the threat of liquid explosives. Each container of liquids, aerosols or gels in your carry-on baggage must be one hundred millilitres or three and a half fluid ounces or less. All the containers must be sealed in a transparent, one litre or thirty-two fluid ounce plastic bag. You are only allowed one bag. Any resealable bag of one litre or thirty-two fluid ounce capacity or less is allowed.

You can carry prescription medicines, baby products and non prescription medicines that you need for the flight. Proof of need may be required. When you get to the screening point, you will have to surrender any liquids or aerosols greater than one hundred millilitres that you still have with you, including duty free. The rules also introduce random frisk searches as part of the screening process. Please prepare your plastic bag before you check in so you will have time to put any containers that are too big into your check in baggage.

The biggest advantages of carry-on luggage only is that you have little chance of it getting lost, stolen, tampered with or broken and once you arrive at your destination, you are on your way while others are waiting at the luggage carousel. You will feel a freedom that most others only dream about.

Another big advantage is the ever increasing cost of travelling with larger pieces of luggage. Just about all airlines now charge for each and every bag that is checked in with the exception of overseas travel, where your first bag is generally free. However, once you land overseas, expect to pay for your bag on all domestic flights, even if you only have one.

So the question is, "Just how do I pack lightly?" Again, you need to be brutally honest with yourself. Firstly, lay out on your bed or a table, everything that you are planning on taking away on your holiday. Now, thinking about the things you will be doing on your holiday and where you will be going, you need to pick up each and every item and ask the question, 'Will I use this item enough times to justify carrying it around with me for the entire time I will be away?' I once carried a ski bag with ski's and poles and a boot bag with ski boots all over America for five weeks, getting charged for excess baggage every time I boarded an aircraft. Out of the thirty five days I was travelling I only skied about ten days. Sometimes it is cheaper and much simpler to just hire gear when you get there. I also do the same thing whenever I go SCUBA diving. I hire equipment near the dive site and will usually buy a mask and snorkel, which I give away before continuing on with my journey. I no longer want to be carrying extra stuff around that I am not using most days.

> 66   *Try and stick to the same colour tones so that you don't have to carry so many pairs of shoes and you can mix and match your outfits.*   99

You also need to think about what you will be wearing. Try and stick to the same colour tones so that you don't have to carry so many pairs of shoes and you can mix and match your outfits. Use accessories to make your clothes look different, rather than taking a lot of different outfits. This can be done with jewellery, scarves, ties and belts.

If you are going to be away for several weeks, you will need to think about washing facilities. In Australia, New Zealand and the United States it is very easy to find coin operated laundromats while in Europe it is almost impossible to find one. Wherever possible, travel with clothes that are light enough to dry quickly overnight and carry a small fold-up washing line with you so that if need be, you can hand wash in your hotel room. Katmandu Stores have one of the best ranges of travel clothes and accessories.

If you are travelling in winter, it is always easier to dress in layers and have just one coat that will go with whatever you are wearing, rather than packing lots of different winter wear which is bulky.

When it comes to actually packing your bag, there are lots of theories on which is the best way. Some people like to flat pack while others prefer to roll and others like to use what is called 'packing cubes' or airless baggies. Whichever method you use, it is always good to keep certain things together so that you can find them easily and grab them quickly if you need to. I have one small bag with two compartments that I keep all my cords and adaptors in. One side has everything I need for my camera including a spare battery and memory cards while the other side holds the cords, chargers and adaptors I need for my tablet and phone. The joy of using the same brand products, whatever that brand might be, is that often the same charger and cords can be used for both. I have another small bag that holds my GPS unit and its charger, and also a charger I can plug into the cigarette lighter socket of any vehicle.

For me, when travelling, I like a mixture of packing cubes and rolling. I like to be able to see exactly where everything is and to be able to grab whatever I need quickly. I also always pack the same things in the same spots within my bag. After so many years of travelling, I don't even have to think about this anymore and can pack a bag in just a few minutes because I know where everything goes and fits. Whether I am packing for a weekend or a one month tour, I pack exactly the same.

Always remember that there is a very high likelihood that you will buy souvenirs, clothes or books on your travels to bring home. Anything extra adds to the weight of your bags.

Below is a checklist of things you may need while you are away. Pack only what you are sure you will need and don't take extra things *just in case*. You can print this list and check off what you need for each holiday or trip by going to my website: www. travellingmadeeasy.com.au

CLOTHING

BEDTIME

Pyjamas			
Nightgown			
Lingerie			
T Shirt			
Boxer Shorts			

DRESSES

Sun Dress			
Short Dress			
Cocktail Dress			
Evening Dress			
Skirt			
Sarong			

PANTS

Long Pants			
Dress Slacks			
Shorts			
Cargo Shorts			
Exercise Shorts			
Sweat Pants			
Jeans			

FORMAL WEAR

Evening Gown			
Suit			
Tuxedo			
Tie			
Bow Tie			
Belt			
Dress Shirt			

SHIRTS

Short Sleeve Button Shirt			
Long Sleeve Button Shirt			
Short Sleeve Polo Shirt			
Long Sleeve Polo Shirt			
T Shirt			
Exercise Shirt			
Sleeveless Shirt			
Blouse			
Tank Top			
Turtleneck Shirt			

SWIMMING

Bikini			
Board Shorts			
Swimming Suit			
Sarong			
Microfibre Towel			

SOCKS

Long Socks			
Short Socks			
Sport Socks			
Thick Socks			
Ski Socks			
Stockings			
Tights			
Leggings			

SHOES

Dress Shoes			
High Heels			
Walking Shoes			
Sports Shoes			
Hiking Boots			
Sandals			
Flip Flops			
Slippers			

UNDERWEAR

Briefs			
Bra			
Sports Bra			
Singlet			
T Shirt			
Boxer Shorts			
Underpants			

WINTER WEAR

Thermals			
Long Johns			
Ski Pants			
Ski Jacket			
Vest			
Cardigan			
Fleece			
Jacket			
Gloves			
Winter Boots			
Overcoat			
Raincoat			
Scarf			

HATS

Sun Hat			
Baseball Cap			
Knitted Hat			

ACCESSORIES

Necklace			
Bracelet			
Ring			
Earrings			
Cuff Links			
Watch			

TOILETRIES

HAIR

Shampoo			
Conditioner			
Mousse			
Hair Gel			
Brush			
Comb			

TEETH

Toothbrush			
Toothpaste			
Dental Floss			
Mouthwash			

BODY

Soap			
Deodorant			
Moisturiser			
Shaver			
Shaving Cream			
Perfume			
Aftershave			
Cologne			

MAKEUP

Face Foundation			
Face Powder			
Lipstick			
Mascara			
Eye Shadow			
Eye Liner			
Makeup Remover			

OTHER ITEMS

Glasses			
Reading Glasses			
Sun Glasses			
Contact Lenses			
Contact Lens Cleaner			
Eye Drops			
Nail Clippers			
Nail File			
Tweezers			
Chap Stick			
Nail Polish			
Nail Polish Remover			
Tampons			
Sanitary Pads			

GADGETS

Laptop Computer			
iPad			
iPod			
MP3 Player			
Headphones			
Mobile Phone			
Kindle			
GPS			
Portable Hard Drive			
Chargers			
Electrical Adapters			
Plug Converter			
USB Storage			
Alarm Clock			
Translator			
Flashlight			
Headlamp			
Binoculars			
Playing Cards			
Book			
Map Book			

Digital Camera			
Macro Lens			
Zoom Lens			
Extra Digital Camera Battery			
Video Camera			
Tripod			
Notebook			
Pocket Knife			
Pen			

CHAPTER 9

STAYING IN TOUCH

CHAPTER 9

STAYING IN TOUCH

> 66 *Modern technology has given us the gift of staying close even though thousands of miles separate us.* 99

Tarnya Hawkins

There are now so many different ways to keep in touch with each other that it can be quite confusing. Apart from sending letters and postcards, most of the ways we keep in touch are by modern technology in the form of emails, messaging, social media video chatting and phone calls. If you are using technology based communication you will need to be connected to the internet or to a phone carrier. Depending on where in the world you are travelling, will determine the usefulness of this modern technology. Some places just do not have internet or mobile phone coverage while other areas may have internet that is so unreliable or slow you can barely use it.

I would suggest that if you have a smart phone and you need to keep in touch while you are away, then take your phone with you. A new rule to be aware of is that when going through security screening in some countries, you need to be able to show the security officer that you can turn your phone on. This is so that they can make sure it is a phone and not an explosive device. Make sure the battery is charged to be able to do this or you risk losing your phone. While we may find all the security measures frustrating, remember these are for your own safety. Once through security, remember to turn off data roaming before you leave your home country or do what I do and take the SIM card out altogether. When I travel, I use my smart phone for most things that I need to do and for keeping in touch. I can preload maps and then use the phone GPS feature without data connection. I can send and receive emails, use FaceTime, send messages and use Facebook. If I have emails to send, I write these ahead of time and then connect to send. I also find the easiest thing for me to do when travelling is to buy a data plan at my destination. You can also buy an international plan from your home phone store or use a company called Travel Sim.

Whichever way you decide to go, you will need to make sure your phone has the right radio frequency. To find out this information ring your phone provider or take your phone into your local store. Basically, phones use one of two options. GSM [Global System for Mobile] communications is the one used the most throughout the world. This is what I use in Australia, Canada and the United States and most other countries I visit. I can simply switch a SIM card and be compatible with the country I am travelling in. CDMA

[Code Division Multiple Access] works in fewer countries. If you have a new phone, chances are that it will have both GMS and CDMA built into it and therefore you can use your own phone in any country you might visit. You could also use your smart phone without buying any data by using any free Wi-Fi hotspots. Most hotels offer free Wi-Fi as part of your nightly rate but there are hundreds of other locations as well. Most airports and a multitude of restaurants and cafes offer free Wi-Fi to entice you to eat there. Be very aware however that free Wi-Fi offered to the public is not generally the safest, so change your password often and don't access any sensitive accounts such as your bank while using public internet sites.

If you want to send messages or speak to someone, iPhone has a built in app called FaceTime. However, you can only use this if you are speaking with someone who also has an iDevice as well. For everyone else you could use the apps Viber or Skype for calling and WhatsApp for texting. I personally like Viber because I can call a landline for a small preloaded fee and for friends who also have the Viber App it is free.

Facebook is also a quick and easy way to keep in touch with anyone, anywhere in the world, who also has a Facebook account. It is also a quick and easy way to send photos. However, be very aware of your privacy settings or your photos or information can be left vulnerable for the whole world to see and access. You can also set up private groups within your account. This is helpful if you only want to stay in touch with family and close friends. For extra security you can make this what is called a 'secret' group so that only those in the group actually see what you are posting.

> 66 *If you have an iPad with a SIM card, you will also need to turn off the data roaming on this device.* 99

Another option is to buy a phone card from the country you are travelling in and use this to call either locally or internationally. Make sure you look at the different options because different cards will have different call rates and some have a connection fee every time you make a call. These come with different plans starting from as low as five dollars and going up to one hundred dollars. They can also have more funds added if you are making more calls than you thought. They do have an expiration date and any credit that you have not used is not refunded.

If you have an iPad with a SIM card, you will also need to turn off the data roaming on this device. It works in the same way as the phone and you may come home to a hefty invoice to pay. You can also obtain prepaid data SIM cards in the various countries you may travel through.

When it comes to sending postcards I use a program called SendOutCards as this allows me to take my own photo, upload it into the program, use my own words and have someone else figure out the postage and take it to the post office for me. My friends get a real postcard that is delivered quickly and I can even send a hundred at a time, all personalised, all done in a matter of minutes. I also use this system for sending my Christmas cards that all have amazing photos of my past year's travels. It has even gotten me out of trouble a few times when I am overseas and remember a birthday that is coming up. Not only can I send a card but also a gift. Check it out at sendoutcards.com/tarnyahawkins

While this is an MLM company, you do not have to join the business to use it as a pay-as-you-go customer.

HOLIDAY PHOTOS AND OTHER INTERESTING THINGS

CHAPTER 10

HOLIDAY PHOTOS AND OTHER INTERESTING THINGS

> 66 *A photo taken is a visual memory of a unique moment in time never to be experienced again. It is the catalyst to you sharing the reality of how you see and experience the world.* 99

Kerri Setch

Over the years I have always carried a camera with me on any of my travelling adventures. Sometimes I have been a super photo-enthusiast and lugged around a heavy DSLR camera, lenses, flash units, filters and so on. Other times I have been more laid back in my approach and been content with using a compact camera or even my phone. Ultimately, it doesn't matter what sort of equipment I pack, rather, it's about having a visual account of my journeys and capturing some unique or cliché or special moments and having the photos to rekindle memories and enhance the retelling of my travels to anyone who will listen when I return.

Just as you will be thinking about your must-see, must-try, must-do and must-visit lists as you plan, pack, go and enjoy, it is worth your while to apply the PPGE (plan, pack, go, enjoy) thought-process to all things photographic. This can be as simple or as complex as you make it.

In the planning of your travels, you will at some point make a decision, either consciously or otherwise, whether you plan to take photos and how you might do that. If you are either someone who doesn't usually take photos or are not confident of your photographic skills – READ ON! It can be more fun than you realise.

Congratulations, you have made the decision to take photos on your travel adventure.

Now that we are in the digital age, the capture and volume of photos captured is more readily accessible once you have the equipment. So, some questions to consider in relation to travel photos and in readiness for your upcoming travels are:

1. Do I have a camera? Will I use it? Do I know how to use it?

2. Do I want to invest in a new camera for this trip? Do I have time to become familiar with how it works?

3. I don't usually take many photos, so will my phone/mobile device be enough?

4. Do I think my current camera will serve me well on this trip?

5. Do I want to take videos or stills or both?

In answering these questions, you may find it helpful to keep your trip in mind. For example, try asking yourself something like:

"When I visit Paris and am standing in front of the Eiffel Tower, do I want to have a photo of this to show my friends or family?"

Or

"When I am exploring the markets in Marrakesh and I see some food that is indescribable and totally not in my regular diet, do I want to be able to show people back home or post it on one of the many social media formats?"

PLAN

If you currently own a camera and haven't used it for quite a while, it will be helpful for you to spend some time before you leave to retrieve it from the depths of the cupboard, blow off the dust and cobwebs and reacquaint yourself with this old friend. Check that it still works and that you are happy with the results.

> 66 *I can offer three helpful words of wisdom to consider when purchasing a new camera - research, research and research.* 99

If it is not functioning or you are unsure of its reliability and you don't want to invest in a new camera, then it is possible to have your camera serviced. You might want to consider this. Refer to your local phone directory or the internet for camera service and/ or repairs businesses. If you have difficulty locating someone in your local area, then you might be able to get some advice from a local camera retailer. Another option would be to contact the service department of the maker of your camera.

I can offer three helpful words of wisdom to consider when purchasing a new camera - research, research and research.

1. Research your options via people you know.

    When connecting with people you respect and trust, talk to them about your trip and your pending decision about taking photos. Ask what camera they have or what they take when they go on travel adventures. Have a look at their pictures and see if you like the quality – bearing in mind of course they may or may not be a 'brilliant photographer' themselves.

2. Research your options via reputable camera retailers.

It has been my experience that retail assistants generally have a passion for photography and an understanding of what cameras will be best suited to your requirements. Their outlet cabinets are stocked with a variety of cameras to suit a range of budgets and levels of ability so it is a fantastic way to see, touch and feel your potential purchase.

3. Research your options via the internet.

You might find researching on the internet helpful before visiting a retail outlet, so that you are slightly informed about your options however, going to the internet after talking with retailers is also a good move as you can find out more information about a few particular models or even if there is a price variance. There are many, many forums with loads of opinions, so this is where you will need to rely on your own instincts about the way forward.

A quick search on the statement, "How to buy a camera" yielded me 268,000,000 answers in 0.35 seconds! Don't let this deter you from making a decision. Use it to your benefit. Another search, which may be a good starting point, is, "Camera Reviews."

At the end of this process, you will be able to make an informed decision weighing up what camera appeals to you, budget, level of interest, degree of user-friendliness, how heavy it is and of course, if it comes in your favourite colour. Don't get caught up in information overload – filter the advice you receive from family, friends, colleagues, retail staff and internet searches to see what you think will best suit you.

Helpful Hint: If purchasing a camera, batteries, memory cards, cases etc. from a retail outlet, remember to ask the question, "Is this your best price?"

Another Helpful Hint: To preserve the longevity of your memory card, format the card to the camera. If you do not know how to do this, or cannot find it in the instruction manual, ask the shop assistant at the camera retail outlet for help.

I have not wanted to confuse you with the many options of cameras on the market, as the choice is quite personal. Many cameras today have the capability to capture video as well as photographs. Increasingly, more cameras are incorporating Wi-Fi capability. This enables you to upload photos directly from your camera to the internet and many of the social media formats such as Facebook, Instagram, Twitter, Flickr or whatever the latest one is.

If you think you want to make a movie of your travels, then it may be more beneficial to consider using a camcorder or GoPro. Important factors to consider if using these devices or something like them, is the quality of the video that will result and its battery life. Charged spare batteries are always handy to have in your daypack.

> 66 *In cold climates, the battery life will be shorter than in warmer climates.* 99

Helpful Hint: In cold climates, the battery life will be shorter than in warmer climates. Sometimes it can be helpful to keep the spare battery in your pocket where it will be kept a bit warmer by your body heat.

When I travel, my faithful laptop goes with me. At the end of each day I do the following in relation to my photos:

1.   Download them to my laptop

2.   Backup/copy to a portable hard drive

3.   Upload a few to Facebook to keep in touch with family and friends.

If I have a lot of spare time and the inclination, I will start to select my favourite shots and copy them to a favourites folder so that when I get home I am ready to show them off or use one of the many online options or SendOutCards, for making a photobook.

On future trips I plan to upload my photos to one of the many cloud storage options such as Dropbox.

This is another decision you will have to make – do I want to carry a laptop or netbook with me? If you decide not to do this, then I suggest that you take additional memory cards so that you have enough space to capture your experiences. Depending on where you are travelling to, will also determine whether you need to take everything with you or whether you will be able to purchase additional memory cards along the way. Be prepared and know that occasionally memory cards can be faulty, so a spare never goes astray. I have found Sandisk to be the most reliable and whilst they may cost a little more, I am confident that they will serve me well.

If you make the decision to use a mobile device such as a phone or tablet, then backing up your images should not be as complicated. Access the Wi-Fi (hopefully free) available at your hotel and save them to Dropbox or whatever your favourite cloud storage is. Alternatively, if there is an internet café nearby, you should be able to transfer your images through their computers.

Helpful Hint: It's not until you have lost all your photos that you realise that making a copy saves a lot of heartache.

PACK

If you are looking for ease of travel, then it is likely you will pack less than others in relation to camera gear. If you are right into heaps of gear for every situation, then you will have to consider more carefully what you are going to take and how you are going to pack. Remember, there are weight restrictions for carry-on baggage. I would suggest that you always carry your camera when travelling on planes. Firstly, it decreases the risk of damage. Secondly, if your luggage goes on a different trip from you, you won't be left without a camera.

Outlined below is a checklist to guide you in your choices. Imagine reaching your tropical island paradise to discover that you left the memory cards at home. It may be that you won't require all of the equipment and accessories listed below, but treat the list as a memory prompter.

☐   Camera, camcorder, video camera, Go Pro, mobile device

☐   Batteries

☐   Battery charger

- ☐ Travel power adapter

- ☐ Memory cards

- ☐ Lens cleaning cloth

- ☐ Travel or mini-tripod (depends how keen you are)

- ☐ Card reader

- ☐ Cable to connect camera to laptop

- ☐ Camera bag or case to protect equipment in case of unexpected dropping of camera/device

- ☐ Waterproof case or shower cap from hotel to protect camera from rain

- ☐ Laptop/netbook and power cable

- ☐ Portable hard drive

GO

Now the fun begins. It may seem like you have spent a lot of time researching as well as practicing to use your camera and download photos (get the photos out of the camera), but let me reassure you that having put the effort in, you will now be able to have fun and capture photos with greater ease. It will inspire you to take more photos than you thought you would because you are familiar with your equipment and it's not so daunting to use it.

If you are visiting cultures significantly different from your own, please be mindful and respectful. In your planning you may have read about the places you will visit so be aware of cultural differences. For example, some temples require your skin to be covered, so it may be necessary to wear a sarong to cover your legs. Your travel agent should also be able to advise you of any cultural differences you may need to be aware of.

I love travel photography and observing the cultural differences of daily life. However, if someone says they don't want me to take their photo I respect that and move on. Attempt to have a conversation with people prior to taking their photo, and then ask permission. A smile goes a long way in building the bridge between the subject and yourself. They may seek some monetary gain for the opportunity and then you have to decide whether you wish to take the photo or not. If you are using a digital camera, show them the picture after you have taken it.

Due to the increased global issue of child-trafficking you need to be careful not to take photos of children without the consent of parents or guardians. Also, most countries these days are sensitive about photos being taken of government buildings. Sometimes these buildings are obvious but be aware that photographing some buildings can draw the attention of police. If there is a sign that says no photos/cameras, respect it or you could find yourself unexpectedly fined or detained.

> *Due to the increased global issue of child-trafficking you need to be careful not to take photos of children without the consent of parents or guardians.*

Helpful Hint: Remember to take your camera with you. It is not much use to you if it's left on the table in the hotel for the day. You never know what you will see or special moments you will experience with your travelling companions that will become a unique moment in time.

ENJOY

One of the greatest pleasures in taking photos whilst travelling is that you can let others see what you have seen. If you want to do a quick edit on your photos, I use the Snapseed app – it's lots of fun and can really change your snapshots into interesting photos. I also like to use CollageIt 3 Pro for making a collage of several photos from the one place. You could create a collage for each day of your travels or every town/city/country you visited or every coffee you drank. This app is a lot of fun – you can add text and save it as a photo which you can then upload to social media.

You can take your photos and retell your trip like dot-points in a list. For example, this is the Eiffel Tower, this is the Tower of London, this is Big Ben, this is the rice field near our hotel, this is, this is, this is …

Alternatively, you can think of your photographic captures in terms of a visual storytelling of the trip of your lifetime. From your early days in education you might remember that a good story has a beginning, a middle and an end. Approach your photo taking in a similar fashion. When you are on tour and you stop for a photo opportunity, or you are strolling around a city and discovering it for yourself, remember this:

1. The beginning – a photo showing the whole area (wide angle shot) capturing the vista that is before you;

2. The middle – parts of the scene that catch your eye (possibly zoom in a bit or walk a bit closer) – this could be market stalls under the Eiffel Tower, or a boat on the water's edge rocking gently on the ebb and flow of the tide; and

3. The end – finer details that you discover as you look closer and not only see with your eyes but with your heart/instinct (zoom in closer or go right up to the market seller and their goods)

Whilst you are on your travels you might notice that there are many brightly coloured houses or the architecture is significantly different in every town you visit or everyone wears decorative hats, so you might decide to include this in your photos. This can be added as a theme to your photos, just as sub-plots get added to stories. Become aware of what you are seeing and you will be amazed.

Helpful Hint: Before you leave, do an internet search on, "How to take good travel photos." My search returned me 244,000,000 in 0.39 seconds. See this as a great way to discover something you may not have considered before.

Helpful Hints: Editing your photos as you take them may seem like a great idea, BUT will use a lot of your battery life.

Each morning, make the first photo you take, one of your hotel or where you slept the night before. When you go back to look at your photos, you have an anchor point for when the photos were taken.

Everything I learned about taking great photos I learned from my good friend Kerri Setch. She and I took our first photographic holiday to the USA and Canada when we were in our early twenties. She now owns her own photographic business and helps hundreds of people take great photos with any sort of camera. Get in touch with Kerri at www.look@kerrisetch.com.au.........and tell her Tarnya said to look after you.

As mentioned earlier in this chapter, there are many options for what to do with your photos, rather than having them left on a memory card and forgotten about until the next trip.

Some options are:

1. Have photos printed at a local camera retailer or department store then put in an album

2. Create your own coffee table book by using online providers

3. Create a slideshow with free software, usually included with your computer

4. Copy your favourite photos to a mobile device and have the flexibility to show your photos if the opportunity arises

5. Save your favourite photos to a USB stick and watch them on your TV

6. Have some photos enlarged, framed and hung on your wall

7. Carry your computer with you everywhere you go and show everyone every photo you made!

So there you have it, plan well to allow yourself the fun of capturing your travels.

INSIDER TIPS AND TRICKS

CHAPTER 11

INSIDER TIPS AND TRICKS

> *Learn from the pain and experiences of others. Do your research! Tips and tricks when travelling can save you thousands of dollars and a lot of heartache.*

Di Hillman

I've been travelling for a long time now and been to just about every country in the world and there are a heap of tricks and tips I've learnt along the way but I'm still learning. On my very last tour I had a fellow traveller share a couple of things that I had never even thought of. Because we were staying in a different hotel almost every night of a three week tour, he took a photo of the hotel name and his room number when he arrived. That way when he went out exploring he could easily find his way back to the hotel and his room without any difficulty or having to write down or remember this information.

Here are a few more tips that you might find helpful; in no particular order.

Passport Expiry

Check your passport regularly to make sure it is still current. There is nothing as devastating as turning up at the airport to find your passport has expired. I could add to that, to know where your passport is. There is nothing so frustrating as not being able to find it the day before you travel. You will also need to make sure that you still have six months left on your passport, from the day you arrive home, before it expires. I find this a ridiculous rule......surely a few weeks would be sufficient. However, I don't make the rules, so make sure you don't get caught out.

Pack Light

Carry-on luggage only should become your goal when travelling. You'll never lose your luggage or have to wait ages at the baggage carousel and you save a lot of dollars not having to pay for checked bags. You will also be able to move around so much more easily when you only have one bag. Checking your bag can add about an hour to your trip.

Internet Friendly Device

Carry some sort of internet device that can pick up free Wi-Fi. Free Wi-Fi points are found all over the world, particularly at airports and hotels and lots of restaurants. Tap into these as it is expensive to use dedicated internet places. Make sure you use legitimate sites and not rogue connections.

A good hotel is any that has free Wi-Fi.

Kindle Instead of Books

If you love to read while you are travelling or on holidays, then use a Kindle. You can load all your favourite books before you go and won't have to lug around those bulky and heavy paperbacks.

Carry a Sarong

The most versatile piece of clothing ever, which can also be used as a towel, a skirt, a dress, to lie on at the beach, to help keep you a bit warmer, to help you not get sunburned, as an emergency bandage, to cover your shoulders and arms when entering a temple and even as a curtain if you need some privacy.

Pack a Small Magnet

As you are checking out of your hotel for the last time, take your magnet and run it up and down the magnetic strip on the back of your hotel key. When you checked in, all your information, including your credit card details, were stored on the card. The magnet will erase all this information. Just remember not to carry this magnet in your wallet or near any of your own cards as it may erase these as well.

Don't Carry a Lot of Cash

I haven't been to one country in the last 10 years that doesn't have ATM machines so you only need to carry enough cash for a few days. You will need to check with your bank about daily withdrawal limits and what transaction fees are charged.

Pack a Deck of Cards

Playing cards will make the time go quicker if you have a delay, they take up so little room and they can bring people together.

Carry an Old Wallet

If you are mugged you can give them this old wallet. Leave an out of date credit card and just a small amount of money in it.

Yell FIRE!

Don't yell help if you get in trouble, yell fire. It's attracts attention faster.

Carry Earplugs

You never know when you will need some peace and quiet. Being able to sleep in an airplane or in a noisy hotel room if your roommate is snoring is a skill not many of us have. If you can afford it, travel with a set of good quality noise cancelling headphones. Get ones that are rechargeable. Choose ones that work for phoning, Skype, aircraft, tablets, listening to music etc.

Choose a Special Diet when Flying

An Asian vegetarian option means you will get your meal first, it will be fresh and not stodgy and will have been made individually rather than mass produced, almost guaranteeing better quality ingredients.

Hold the Ice

If you are travelling through a country where you shouldn't drink the water, have your drinks without ice. Also remember to use bottled water for brushing your teeth and keep your mouth closed while swimming and showering.

Travel on Your Own

This might sound like a terrible idea but you will find you talk to more people, immerse yourself more in the local culture and customs and even learn more of local languages. I've met friends for life while I have been travelling on my own.

Take a Limo

Take all the stress out of getting to the airport on time and back from the airport at the end of your trip by booking a limo service. If there are a number of you travelling this usually works out cheaper than a shuttle service and is heaps more comfortable and enjoyable.

Double Check Whenever you Leave

Make sure you always do a double check of the room you have stayed in or any place where you have been sitting. That way you won't leave anything behind.

Pack Things in the Same Place

I always pack things into exactly the same location, whether that is my luggage, my backpack or even my pockets. This way I know immediately if something is missing.

Sleep Like a Local

To avoid jet lag, do not go to sleep during the day of your arrival, even if you have just flown for thirty hours without sleep. Wait until night and go to sleep at the local time.

Take a Road Trip

If you really want to learn about a country, drive across it. Your holiday becomes an adventure. Flying just makes it a trip.

Be an Adventure Traveller not a Destination Traveller

Destination travellers just want to get from Point A to Point B as quickly as possible. Adventure travellers know that the journey from Point A to Point B is what travelling is all about.

No One Likes an Ugly Tourist

No one cares if everything is bigger and better where you come from. There is no excuse for being rude, loud or obnoxious. People will avoid you and you give your home country a bad name.

Use the Same Type of Battery

If at all possible have the same type of battery in all your gadgets.

Self Medication

Carry some Tiger Balm and a pack of Dr Po Chai [found in any Asian grocery store]. These two commodities will get you out of trouble for most ailments.

USB Storage

Copy itinerary, passports, tickets, essential home phone numbers, insurance etc. onto a USB and take it with you. You can also photocopy all your details and swap storage of these with your travel partner.

Carry-on Luggage

Pack one set of lightweight clothes, including underwear, in your carry-on luggage.

Keep it All Together

Use lightweight draw string bags to keep small items of clothing and other personal items together. There will also be no embarrassment when asked to open your bag for customs.

The Gadget Kit

Keep all your computer cords and gadgets in the one small bag. I have another small bag [these can be pencil cases] that I only keep all my camera gear in.

Travelling with a Guitar

If you travel with a guitar and buy too many things, you can take the strings off the guitar and stuff clothes inside it. However, if customs wants to unpack everything and you have put your worn underwear and socks inside the guitar, none of you will enjoy the experience. Plus, the guitar will only be suitable for playing the blues afterwards. True story from a trip to Thailand in 1984, for my friend Craig.

Water Access

If you are on a driving holiday, buy a tap head. This way you can access water in places where the tap head has been removed to avoid water wastage.

Running Shoes

Always pack a pair of super light running shoes. You'll find a use for these on every trip.

Spectacles

Travel with spectacles that are bifocal and turn into sunglasses outside. Get them to safety spec standard as well. It saves having to carry multiple sets of glasses.

Cleaning up Spills

If you drip something on to your top, you can easily remove this by using a small hand wipe, like the type they give you when you are eating chicken, or a baby wipe works just as well.

Laundry Detergent

There is no need to carry laundry detergent for washing by hand; shampoo works just as well.

Carry Water

Always carry a bottle of drinking water in your backpack.

While Travelling

Lip balm, eye drops and a neck pillow can provide comfort on a long journey, particularly if you are in an aircraft.

Overnight Stays

Only unpack what you need from your bag for the amount of time you are staying.

Get Ready the Night Before

Organise your clothes, shoes, day pack, camera etc. the night before for the following day. The next morning you will only need to pack your sleepwear and toiletries before you are ready to leave. Ideal if you have overslept!

Weigh Your Bag

Before deciding which bag to take on your trip, weigh it. Some bags weigh up to five kilograms before you have packed one single item in them.

Keep it Dry

For any activities you do around water, make sure your passport and any other water sensitive items are sealed in some type of waterproof bag. You will need to replace all documents, including your passport, if they are not readable.

CHAPTER 12

TIME TO LEAVE

CHAPTER 12

TIME TO LEAVE

> " *Isn't it interesting that people feel best about themselves right before they go on vacation? They've cleared up all of their to-do piles, closed up transactions, renewed old promises with themselves. My most basic suggestion is that people should do that more than just once a year.* "

David Allen

The big day finally arrives and you have probably had a restless period beforehand, going over all your preparations to ensure that you have not missed anything on your checklist.

You have no doubt considered how much time you should allow yourself to travel to the airport and pass through all the obligatory processes prior to getting to your seat on the plane.

One thing you can be pretty much assured of – your plane will almost certainly leave very close to its scheduled departure time.

Aircraft cost a lot more to airlines when they are sitting idle on the tarmac waiting, than when they are in the air.

When I travel, I count back from the published departure time and allow myself sufficient time for check-in delays, clearance though security and customs (including any queuing delays etc.), last minute duty free purchases etc. plus known travel time from home to the airport.

Airlines and government agencies, including customs, recommend that for wide body aircraft (Boeing 747, Airbus A380, Boeing 777 etc.) passengers should be at the international terminal about three hours in advance of departure time.

For smaller narrow body aircraft (Boeing 737, Airbus A320 etc.) allow two and a half hours in advance of departure.

So, for example, for a B747 flight to Los Angeles departing at 9.00 a.m I would aim to be at the airport around 6.00 a.m. For a B737 flight to Auckland departing at say 11.00 a.m, I would aim for 8.30 a.m.

Upon arrival at the terminal, locate your check-in counter and proceed directly there to offload that bulky check-in baggage. Once completed, you have time to say your goodbyes to any family and friends who have come along to help enjoy the thrill of your departure (and maybe put in a last minute order for a small memento of your travels).

You should remember that there may be delays in processing through airport security and customs, so don't delay in proceeding to the security checkpoint. It is here that you will present your clear plastic bag to security screening staff. You will be asked to remove any coat that you are wearing and often, your shoes and belt.

Once through the security checkpoint, you move on to clear customs. You should have the three documents ready that you will be asked for by the customs processing officers:

1. Your passport

2. A completed outgoing passenger card

3. Your airline boarding pass

Note that you should have received a blank outgoing passenger card from your travel agent previously but supplies are on hand at the airport. To avoid delays in going through customs, you must have this card completed prior to your presentation to the customs officer at departures. These cards are available in many languages, including English.

There are certain goods which are illegal to export (and/or import) from Australia and a list of these can be found on the Australian Customs and Border Protection website: www.customs.gov.au

You should have a look at this before you travel.

Helpful Hint: If you have prescription medication, ensure that you have a letter from your doctor on his/her office stationery identifying which drugs you need to have with you. This is helpful both on your departure and arrival from/into Australia and other countries.

Although there is no limit on the amount of currency you can take from or bring into Australia, there are laws which require you to declare any amounts of $10,000 or more in any currency. There is an opportunity for you to declare these on your outward (departing) and inward (arriving) passenger cards.

Note that Australian customs no longer stamp Australian passports as a matter of course but may if you ask them to do so.

Australian customs is presently trialling a new system of processing passengers called eGates. This is a voluntary system where you can choose to be processed at the customs departures and arrivals lines by using document and face scanners in lieu of the traditional face to face process with a customs officer. The system is very easy to use and may help avoid significant queuing delays if you want to give it a go. It is currently available for travellers on board select Qantas and Air New Zealand flights but will be expanded in due course.

See the customs website for more details.

Once you have made it through the customs line, you will have the wonders of the outwards/ departures lounge before you. There you will find many duty free shops as well as food outlets and book stores etc. Because you came to the airport well in advance of the departure time, you should have plenty of time to browse or relax prior to boarding your flight.

One counter of obvious interest to you could be the Tourist Refund Scheme counter located in the departures lounge. This is staffed by Australian customs officers and offers refunds of GST (Goods and Services Tax) and WET (Wine Equalisation Tax) paid on some goods purchased in Australia. Conditions apply and a list of those as well the goods on which a refund can be claimed and much more information, can be found at the Tourist Refund Scheme applications webpage.

Note that Australia is one of the few countries in the world that offers its citizens a refund of such local taxes. Normally, refunds are only offered to visiting tourists.

The sting in the tail to using the scheme is that you will need to declare all goods for which you obtained a refund if you have them with you upon return to Australia. The value of the goods will be taken into account when you claim your passenger concessions. See the website for more details.

CHAPTER 13

WHEN THINGS DON'T GO ACCORDING TO PLAN

CHAPTER 13

WHEN THINGS DON'T GO ACCORDING TO PLAN

> *Adventure is a path. Real adventure — self-determined, self-motivated, often risky — forces you to have firsthand encounters with the world. The world the way it is, not the way you imagine it. Your body will collide with the earth and you will bear witness. In this way you will be compelled to grapple with the limitless kindness and bottomless cruelty of humankind — and perhaps realise that you yourself are capable of both. This will change you. Nothing will ever again be black-and-white.*

Mark Jenkins

I have a passenger who travels with me on my small group tours. He has been the owner of many different businesses over the years and as the owner, if there was a problem, then he was the one who had to fix it. His thinking these days goes something like this. If I'm going on an extended holiday, somewhere during that time something is bound to go wrong or not to plan. If I only travel on a fully escorted tour, then that problem will never be mine to deal with. I can relax and it is up to the tour leader to get the problem fixed.

For some of you reading this book, your thoughts will be the same. It is perhaps one of the best reasons ever for going off on a holiday where all the work is done for you and you have to do nothing except enjoy yourself and decide what photo's to take or what to eat, while you enjoy your holiday, knowing everything will be taken care of for you.

However, if you are making all the decisions for your holiday then these next pages might help you avoid some of the pitfalls that lead to common travel disasters.

Make sure you have travel insurance. If you can't afford travel insurance, then you can't afford a holiday. Make this a part of your budget when you are planning your trip. If you travel more than a couple of times a year it might be more economical to get a travel insurance policy that lasts for twelve months. Make sure you read all of the fine print and be very clear about what your policy covers before you purchase a policy. Some credit card providers will automatically give you travel insurance if you spend over $500 towards your trip using your credit card. Be very careful of these policies and ask your provider to send out a statement confirming what is actually covered. I had one client pay for a very expensive holiday to Canada and Alaska including numerous rail journeys. She had quickly read most of the policy her bank provided [it was over thirty pages long] and thought she was covered for everything. When her Aunty suddenly got very sick a week out from her departure date, she needed to cancel her trip to look after things at home, including organising the funeral as my client was power of attorney and executor of her estate. When she contacted the insurance provider she was told that she was not covered as her Aunty was older than eighty years. My advice is to make sure you read all the pages and especially any fine print.

ILLNESS AND INJURY

From a mild cold to that tummy ache known as 'bali belly' or a broken limb from a slip on snow or ice, nearly all travellers experience some discomfort at some time or other. Sometimes it is impossible to avoid but there are ways to decrease your chances of getting sick or having an injury.

- Before your holiday, load up on vitamins, especially vitamin C, drink plenty of water and get some decent sleep in the week leading up to your trip.

- Wash your hands as often as you can when taking any form of public transport and especially after using toilets or restrooms. I am constantly horrified by the number of people who I see walk out of a toilet without washing their hands. Apart from this being an unhealthy habit, it is the quickest way to infect yourself and others. ALWAYS wash your hands before you eat anything and avoid touching your face or mouth with dirty hands. Keep sanitiser in your bag or pocket for when water and soap are not available.

- Be smart in your choice of activities. If you have never skied before, don't take a chairlift to the top of a mountain and expect to be able to ski down, just because you are in Switzerland. Tourists get injured every year by doing things that are really stupid. Often times these injuries occur once a substantial amount of alcohol is involved. Be especially cautious where water is concerned. For example, tubing and fooling around in rivers, doing backflips, diving into rivers and even zip lining all have an element of danger. I'm not saying don't do these things, as they are a lot of fun, just don't do them if you've been drinking. If you've never ridden a motorbike before, learning to ride one in Saigon might not be the most sensible thing to do.

- Take care when eating any type of street food. This is one of the great pleasures of travelling, when you get to try the local cuisine of the countries you are visiting and one of the things that I love to do. My rule of thumb is to eat only street food where I can see the food being prepared and cooked in front of me.

- Carry a small first aid kit with you that contains anti diarrhea tablets, a generic antibiotic, antihistamine tablets and perhaps sea sickness tablets if you will be on a ship and suffer from sea sickness. Have a chat with your doctor to see what they think you will need, dependent on your own medical history and the countries you are travelling through.

WHAT TO DO IF YOU GET SICK OR INJURED

If it is something minor, go to a local chemist or pharmacy. Most pharmacies around the world will have a trained chemist in attendance who you can speak with and they can give you advice on over the counter medicines that could cure you without you having to go to a doctor or hospital.

If it is more than just something minor, go to a hospital or doctor. Don't put it off because you think it is going to cost too much. This is why you have travel insurance. Once you see a doctor and receive an indication of what your illness or injury may be, you will need to ring your travel insurance provider immediately and they will advise you on what to do next.

If you are staying at a hotel when you get sick, check with the front desk about local doctors and hospitals. A number of places have a service where the doctor will come to your hotel room and see you. This is especially great if you are in an unfamiliar city.

All cruise ships carry a doctor and have a small hospital clinic on board. If you get sick while cruising, see the doctor as soon as possible. As well as getting better as quickly as possible, you don't want your illness to spread to the rest of the passengers.

LOST LUGGAGE

The second most common thing that goes wrong is that you will arrive at your destination and head to the luggage carousel to collect your luggage only to find, after a very long wait, that your bag has not arrived with you. The best way to avoid this dilemma is to only travel with carry-on luggage. If you are travelling for longer than a couple of days this is just not practical and you will have to check a bag in. Always assume that the airline may lose your luggage and that you will either never get it back or that it may take up to three days for you to be reunited with it. Keep this in mind when you are packing your carry-on luggage. Important documents like your passport, insurance information, itinerary, vouchers for accommodation, tours or rental cars and airline tickets are all packed in your carry-on luggage. Anything of value like credit/debit cards, cash, laptops, expensive jewellery, camera, phone and any other electronic media devices should also be packed in your carry-on luggage. Glasses, contact lenses and medication should be packed and carried with you. Depending on how many gadgets you are taking, room should be left for a change of clothes including underwear. If you are going from a hot to a cold climate or vice versa, make sure you have appropriate clothing in your carry-on.

You will need to make a list of what is in your checked bag as the airline will want to know the specifics of what is in it if it is lost. The best thing is to take a photo of your packed bag, both inside and out. You can show this photo to the airline representative so they know exactly what they are searching for.

WHAT TO DO WHEN YOUR LUGGAGE HAS BEEN LOST

- Remain as calm as possible. It is sometimes easier said than done when you really just want to scream your frustration at someone. The person you will be talking with was not the person who lost your bag but they will be the person to do everything they can to get it back to you, so always remember to be polite. Rudeness will never help anyone.

- Do not leave the airport. As quickly as possible, find the airline counter, submit a report and file a claim immediately. Show the photo [on your phone or camera] of your bag and have your checked bag stub available for the identification number. The airline staff may be able to find it quickly and easily from the information you have just given them.

- Be persistent. You should never be rude but if you are not receiving the service you require, continue until you are completely satisfied.

- If you have paid for your checked in baggage, try and recoup those fees. As crazy as it sounds, not all airlines have to refund your baggage fees even if they have lost your luggage. Make sure you save yourself from feeling even more frustrated by knowing the rules regarding the airline you are flying with.

- Ring your travel insurance provider and follow their instructions as to how they would like you to proceed in replacing your luggage.

BEING ROBBED OR MUGGED

Nowhere is completely safe if you happen to be in the wrong place at the wrong time, not even in your local neighbourhood at home. You could be robbed in the middle of London, Rome, Paris, New York, Rio, Sydney or even Vatican City. You can do a few things though that will keep you safer from potential thieves.

- Wear a money belt. Annoying or as uncomfortable as they can sometimes be, it is almost impossible to pickpocket one.

- Don't carry too many valuables with you. When leaving your hotel or accommodation, just take a small amount of cash with you.

- Use the hotel safety deposit box rather than the safe in your room for added security.

- Keep your hotel room tidy and lock your suitcase before you leave your room. If things are left out all over the place, you wouldn't really know if something went missing.

- Don't draw attention to yourself with flashy jewellery or a big camera around your neck.

- DO NOT wear one of those fanny packs or bum bags. Nothing screams 'tourist' more than these. Try to dress like the locals and blend in. Do you really think an Italian is going to wear board shorts and a loud shirt with running shoes while walking around Rome?

- Ladies, I know you love handbags and carrying purses but these can be easily snatched. If you must carry a bag, make sure it goes across the front of your body, keep it zippered at all times and tucked under the arm away from the street.

- If you are using a small backpack to stow your gear in, wear the back pack on the front of your body if you are in very crowded situations. That way, it can't be opened without your knowledge.

- Never put your bag under your seat, especially on trains or buses.

- Always keep an eye on your belongings. When you are checking in to a hotel or a ticket counter for a bus or train, always keep your gear near you and know where it is at all times.

- Know where you are going. Every city has a bad area and you do not want to end up there by mistake. Keep away from deserted or dimly lit areas and stay where the crowds are. If you start to have a bad feeling about a certain area, leave immediately. Trust your instincts.

WHAT TO DO IF YOU GET ROBBED OR MUGGED

Hopefully you will never have to experience this. However, assuming you are safe and have no injuries, there are a few steps to follow.

- Report immediately to the local police. This can sometimes be as traumatic as the robbery itself, as most times they will do nothing and will often not even seem to care. Remain as calm as possible and file a report and ask for a copy. When you speak to your travel insurance provider about recovering costs on stolen goods, the first thing they will ask for is the police report.

- Call your travel insurance provider and file a claim with them. You will want to get things rolling as soon as possible.

- If your passport was stolen, then you will need to go to the nearest embassy as soon as possible. This can be a frustrating experience but you cannot leave the country you are in until you have a replacement passport.

- Even if your passport was not stolen, you may still have to visit the embassy as they can help you with emergency cash, cancelling your credit card or making phone calls on your behalf.

LOST OR STOLEN PASSPORT

A lost or stolen passport will cause you more grief than almost anything else if you are travelling overseas, so make sure you keep it in a very safe place and know where it is at all times.

Without your passport, it will be impossible for you to leave the country you are in and to get home. Some countries will not check you into a hotel or change money for you without sighting your passport.

Personally, I carry my passport with me in a money belt which I wear at all times. Others on our team at Travelling Made Easy carry a copy of their passport with them and leave their original passport in the safe of the hotel room. So it really is a personal choice with no right or wrong answer. Whatever you decide, make sure you have a copy of your passport in a couple of places so that you can access the information quickly, should it get lost or stolen. I also have a photo of my passport stored on my phone. I would only suggest this if you have a lock on your phone, as mine does.

WHAT TO DO IF YOUR PASSPORT BECOMES LOST OR STOLEN

- Stay calm. You are not the first person and you won't be the last to lose a passport while in a foreign country.

- Find out where your nearest embassy is and go to it as quickly as you can.

- Be prepared as there is a LOT of paperwork to fill out to get a replacement passport. If it was stolen, you will need a police report.

- If you need a replacement passport in a hurry, especially if you need to depart from the county quickly, then you can pay extra to have the process rushed through.

MISSING YOUR FLIGHT

- If you are booking a number of flights on the same day, make sure you have allowed enough time from the time you land to the time you need to board your next flight. Flights invariably run late and often arrive after the scheduled time. Factor this in to your connecting flight and allow enough time for possible delays, enough time to disembark from the aircraft [you may be sitting in the last row] and enough time to get to the next gate [some airports are huge]. If you have to clear immigration and customs before a connecting flight, give yourself a minimum of two hours.

- On the day of travel, make sure you have two ways of waking up. Set an additional alarm, either on your phone, computer or watch or ask for a wakeup call.

- Give yourself plenty of time to get to the airport. Ask how long it will take to get to the airport at the hour you want to travel. What may normally take an hour may take two hours if you are travelling in peak hour traffic. On the way to the airport, an accident, weather or any other unforeseen incident may slow your journey, so give yourself plenty of time. If you arrive early you arrive relaxed and then will have time to look around the shops, people watch or even enjoy a coffee or cold drink.

• Check the departure board. Just because it might say on your boarding pass that you are leaving from Gate 23 doesn't necessarily mean that you do leave from Gate 23. Gate changes happen all the time so check the departure board often in the lead up to your boarding time. When you reach your departure gate, make sure that you check that the flight you are travelling on is correct and displayed. Just this week, as I was boarding a flight to Mackay, the chap ahead of me thought he was boarding his flight to Cairns. There had been a gate change and he didn't check. As my flight to Mackay had been delayed, his flight to Cairns had already departed.

WHAT TO DO IF YOU MISS YOUR FLIGHT

• If the flight you miss is a connecting flight using the same airline or partner airline, it then becomes the airline's responsibility to get you on the next available flight to your destination.

- If, however, you miss your flight due to other reasons like traffic, sleeping in, weather etc. you may have to pay for another flight. Depending on the airline, whether or not you are charged for a new flight can be totally up to the airline employee. This is excellent information to keep in mind as you deal with this person. How you act towards the person at the counter may in some cases determine how much you do or don't pay. Treat them with respect and kindness, bearing in mind that it is not their fault you missed your flight.

- If you are travelling during a busy period, especially holiday times, airlines will overbook. This is because a percentage of passengers do not show up for their flight for one reason or another. However, if everyone does arrive, you will hear airline staff saying the flight is overbooked and they are looking for volunteers to give up their place on the flight and take a later flight. If you can go on a later flight, you can pick up a lot of freebies including another free flight. So take advantage of this and again, being as nice as possible will help your cause.

NATURAL DISASTERS

Natural disasters usually happen without much warning and cannot be avoided. The only precaution is to look at the area you will be travelling to and see if that area is known for natural disasters at a particular time of the year. That way, you can make an informed decision about when you choose to travel there.

Travel insurance before you travel can help cover any financial losses you may incur due to a natural disaster. Do make sure you read all the fine print in your policy to see exactly what you are covered for.

A little known fact about when natural disasters occur, be it a tsunami or a volcanic eruption, if you have booked all your holiday arrangements online, you are pretty much on your own. If you have booked through a reputable travel agent, then you have that agency working for you to do all that is possible to get you home safely. Another myth is that booking online yourself will be a cheaper option. This is rarely true and often in my own business, I can get a better deal or at least the same price for my clients and they travel with the confidence that they have a whole office who can help them out if things go wrong.

WHAT TO DO IF YOU FIND YOURSELF IN THE MIDDLE OF A NATURAL DISASTER

- Firstly, always remain as calm as possible, particularly if you are not hurt. Find the rest of your group and make sure that everyone is safe.

- There is likely to be chaos happening all around you, so don't add to that by panicking, becoming hysterical or getting angry or impatient.

- Electricity and communication means will very likely either not be working or not working very well. This means that you may not be able to communicate with your family back home. They will, more than likely, have heard the news and be worrying about your safety, so if there is a way of communication via phone or internet, let them know that you are safe.

- Some sort of command centre will be set up in a central location. Go to this area to see what is going to happen next. Where you need to go for shelter, if you are likely to be evacuated or even if there is something you can do to help. You may have skills that are required.

Your chances of experiencing any of these problems are very minor and should not deter you from experiencing all that travelling across our beautiful world has to offer. Be prepared and know in the back of your mind what to do if you run into a problem, then enjoy your holiday.

COMING HOME

CHAPTER 14

COMING HOME

> 66 *He who returns from a journey*
> *is not the same as he who left.* 99

Chinese Proverb

The excitement of your big adventure away from home is almost over and has been replaced by perhaps a little anxiety about clearing customs at home. Fear not. This process has been simplified over the recent years and should be very simple, providing you adhere to a few simple and basic rules.

The most important thing to remember is that if you are unsure about anything you have with you or obtained overseas, it is better to declare it to the customs and quarantine officers than not to and risk a penalty.

Penalties can be severe, including large on-the-spot fines and/or possible prosecution or action.

If in doubt, declare it to customs. (Australian Customs and Border Protection Service)

The process upon arriving back home at the international terminal is quite straightforward.

Firstly, when you disembark from your aircraft, you will walk up the relevant arrivals concourse to the entry control point/arrivals processing area. Along the way, you will pass by the inevitable duty free shop. There you will find more duty free items such as perfumes, alcohol and cigarettes to tempt you to spend more of your hard earned dollars. You may have prepaid/ordered some duty free items from the duty free company in the departures hall when you left and these will be packaged and labelled up for you to collect at this point.

The important thing to remember here is not to spend too long in this shop as no doubt other aircraft are arriving with copious loads of passengers and you don't want to be caught up in the inevitable crush of passengers fighting for a place in the queue to be processed by customs. Remember, family and friends are also eagerly awaiting you on the other side of the customs hall.

Another thing to remember about your passenger concessions is that you must include these duty free purchases in your passenger allowance which is currently $900 per adult eighteen years of age and older and $450 per child under eighteen years of age. Families travelling together can pool this allowance. See the customs website for more details.

Next, you will be confronted at the customs processing point. Here you will be required to present your passport and completed incoming passenger card. The blank incoming passenger card should have been provided to you by the cabin crew on your flight and should have been completed by you prior to arrival. Supplies are however available in the customs queuing area if needed, in a great variety of languages.

Make sure you have completed and signed this two sided declaration fully and honestly as it is regarded by the authorities as a legal document and will be presented in court by the authorities if an unfortunate situation results. Read the document carefully and ask the cabin crew on the aircraft or customs officers located in the arrivals hall for their help if you are unsure about anything.

A list of goods which are considered prohibited and restricted imports can be found on the customs website www.customs.gov.au

It would be a good idea to make yourself familiar with these before you leave Australia.

Helpful Hint: Don't be tempted into buying that fake big name handbag, watch or pirated movies etc. whilst overseas. Many big international companies (such as Chanel, YSL, Calloway Golf etc.) are very protective of their brands and reputations and are more than willing to take legal action in Australia against anyone found

to be importing fake and inferior quality reproductions of their big selling items. Australian customs has an obligation to seize these counterfeit goods when they discover them and sometimes will also refer the details of the importer to the company for their further action.

When you approach the customs line, you will be given a choice of either being processed face to face with a customs officer or being self-processed through SmartGate.

SmartGate is an electronic document and facial recognition initiative by the Australian government aimed at speeding up the processing of arriving passengers. The system is available to:

- Australian, New Zealand, United Kingdom, United States of America or Singapore ePassport holders

- Switzerland, Canadian and Irish ePassport holders are also able to use the system, on a trial basis

- Passengers who are aged sixteen years or over or an Australian ten to fifteen years old and travelling with two adults and

- Have arrived at a SmartGate equipped airport

Airports which currently are equipped with SmartGate include:

- Cairns

- Brisbane

- Gold Coast

- Sydney

- Melbourne

- Adelaide

- Perth

- Darwin

Next, you will arrive at the baggage collection carousel and it will be there that you collect your bags. Note that Australian airports do not have baggage porters or staff available to load your bags onto trolleys for you, so be prepared to grab a trolley from the trolley racks and load your own bags onto it. At most airports, the trolleys are free.

Make sure you have all of your baggage and have not left anything behind such as any item the airline might have carried separately on the flight for you, such as golf bags, strollers, wheelchairs, oversized baggage, other sporting goods etc.

You will then be met by a customs officer who will collect your incoming passenger card from you and might ask you some questions about what you have declared or are carrying etc. Note that you could be referred for a baggage x-ray or baggage examination and this is not unusual. Quarantine officers will also be present and will be interested in any food, soil, plant material etc. that you might have. Providing that you have declared all that you have, this should be a simple and brief process.

Then, you will be free to exit the arrivals hall into the waiting arms of those family and friends who can't wait to hear the tales of your recent adventures.

AUTHORS FINAL WORD

"We need to travel. If we don't offer ourselves to the unknown, our senses dull, our world becomes small and we lose our sense of wonder. Our eyes don't lift to the horizon; our ears don't hear sounds around us. The edge is off our experiences and we pass our days in a routine that is both comfortable and limiting. We wake up one day and find we have lost our dreams in order to protect our days. Don't let yourself become one of these people. The fear of the unknown and the lure of the comfortable will conspire to keep you from taking the chances the traveller has to take but if you take them, you will never regret your choice. To be sure, there will be moments of doubt when you stand alone on an empty road in an icy rain or when you are ill with fever in a rented bed but as the pains of the moment will come, so too will they fall away. In the end you will be so much richer, so much stronger, so much happier and so much a better person, that all the risk and no sleep will seem like nothing compared to the knowledge that you have gained."

These words were penned by Brandon Jeffrey, the brother of my good friend Devon Chandler, as he travelled around the world for one year. I hope they will inspire you to travel as much as you are able and to see as many of the places that I have had the privilege of seeing in my lifetime.

ABOUT THE AUTHOR

TARNYA HAWKINS

Entrepreneur, Investor, Author, Charity Organiser and World Traveller

Tarnya is a successful entrepreneur, lifelong charity volunteer and organiser, chef, athlete, investor, author and world traveler.

Her love of travel began at an early age and led to her many accomplishments in the travel industry. Tarnya began travelling at the age of fifteen while working on cruise ships. Now she operates a leading travel company that offers ocean and river cruising, coach tours across Australia, sailing adventures including regatta's and specified small group tours. Her favourite tours to lead are throughout Canada, South America and the United States, including Hawaii and Alaska.

She has worked and consulted with a long list of highly respected companies in the travel industry including Integrity Travel, Cross Country Tours, Princess Cruises, Norwegian Cruise Lines, Qantas Holidays, Expedia, SureSave Travel Insurance and Sailing Adventures just to name a few.

Tarnya is also a talented and award-winning chef. As a young twenty year old entrepreneur she started her own catering company and worked with Inflight Catering for six years. Tarnya now blends her love of food and travel into her small group experiences.

Tarnya Hawkins is an international bestselling author. She has travelled to over fifty countries across five continents and has an intimate knowledge of Canada and the United States. Her passion is helping others take amazing travelling adventures and holidays.

In addition to travelling, her interests include cooking, photography, skiing, snowmobiling and her charitable work. Tarnya has been deeply committed to many charitable organisations throughout her life. Over the years she has been involved with drug rehabilitation and suicide prevention programs, organising international youth conferences, conventions, rallies and camping programs that have touched the lives of many thousands of young people from all over the world. She has also served for many years as a youth and children's minister for the Uniting Church and Anglican Church.

Success Resources

Travelling
Made Easy

To view the full range of tours, visit

www.TravellingMadeEasy.com.au

Change Your Life with Professional Hypnosis CDs

There is a powerful force inside every human being that, once unlocked, can make any dream, vision, or desire become a reality. The Power was given to you at birth and it lives within all of us. Its power is unlimited and all you need to do is capture it. You'll have a life filled with more abundance, passion, excitement, confidence, joy and love than you ever dreamed possible.

Overcoming Fear,
Anxiety & Stress

Overnight Confidence

How To Quit Smoking

Plus many more to choose from.
To find out more, visit

www.TravellingMadeEasy.com.au